Edexcel

DiDA

Diploma in Digital Applications

Multimedia

Kevin Burden

Theo Kuechel

Allan Smith

Contents

Contents

Introduction

Welcome to Multimedia

Congratulations! Now you have completed Unit 1, and maybe other units of the Diploma in Digital Applications (DiDA), and you are ready to move on to Unit 2.

Unit 2 lets you get to grips with some of the latest, most exciting and creative ways of using ICT. You have already done a lot of the groundwork for this unit in Unit 1. You will find the practical hands-on approach stimulating and rewarding.

This unit will provide you with the skills you need to design and create effective multimedia products. To start with you will investigate existing products to discover more about the potential of multimedia. Then you will learn how to design and produce your own multimedia products. Sometimes you will use existing assets, but you will also learn how to create new ones. Finally, you will bring all the components you have collected together to create a multimedia product.

You will demonstrate your multimedia abilities by working on a project set by Edexcel. You will exhibit this in an eportfolio, which will be a multimedia product in itself.

You can find out more by looking at the specification on Edexcel's website.

A reminder about DiDA

▶ **Award in Digital Applications (AiDA):** If you've already successfully completed Unit 1, you are eligible for this. It is equivalent to one GCSE.

▶ **Certificate in Digital Applications (CiDA):** Successfully completing Unit 1 and Unit 2 (or any one of the other optional units) entitles you to this award. It is equivalent to two GCSEs.

▶ **Diploma in Digital Applications (DiDA):** If you successfully complete Unit 1 and *three* optional units, you are eligible for DiDA. It is equivalent to four GCSEs.

At the moment the optional units are *Unit 2: Multimedia, Unit 3: Graphics* and *Unit 4: ICT in Enterpris*e, but others may be added in the future.

Audience and purpose

One of the key themes in Unit 1 was the importance of producing publications that are right for the intended audience. This is just as important for multimedia products. So how do you do this?

The key questions you need to ask yourself are:

▶ **Who** is it for?
▶ **Why** is it needed?
▶ **Where** is the audience?
▶ **What** must go in it?

Answering these questions will help you to identify exactly what you are trying to achieve. Once you've done this you can *then* decide:

▶ **How** you are going to go about it.

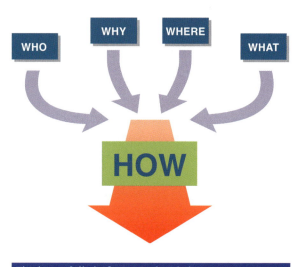

Think carefully before you decide how

How to use the ActiveBook

DiDA is all about digital applications and these materials reflect this. As well as the printed book there is also an ActiveBook. This is on the CD that comes with the book, and you may also be able to view it over your centre's network.

The ActiveBook is a digital version of the paper-based book. The pages look the same, but there is a big difference — it's interactive!

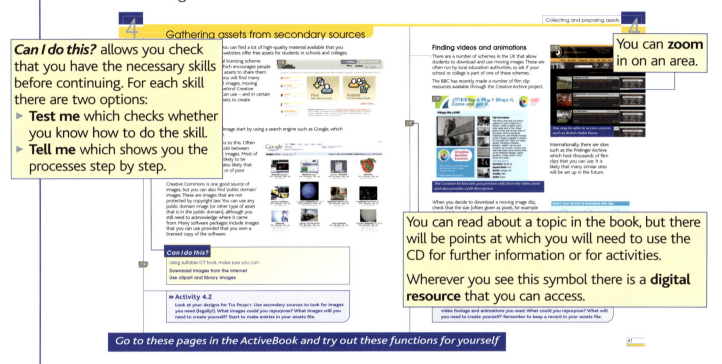

Can I do this? allows you check that you have the necessary skills before continuing. For each skill there are two options:
► **Test me** which checks whether you know how to do the skill.
► **Tell me** which shows you the processes step by step.

You can **zoom** in on an area.

You can read about a topic in the book, but there will be points at which you will need to use the CD for further information or for activities.

Wherever you see this symbol there is a **digital resource** that you can access.

Go to these pages in the ActiveBook and try out these functions for yourself

If you are looking at the ActiveBook on a network, you will also be able to watch the **digimodules** — these are introductory presentations at the start of each chapter.

Assessment

You will remember from Unit 1, and any other DiDA units you have done, that there is no formal exam. Instead you work on a project. The project is described in the Summative Project Brief (SPB), which is published as a website by Edexcel. It gives you the chance to demonstrate the skills you have gained in the unit by developing multimedia products that are creative, effective and fit for purpose. The final stage of the SPB is to create an eportfolio that will allow others to view your publications on screen and to see evidence of how you produced them.

Preparing for the SPB

THE PROJECT is a mini website just like the real SPB. It has the same type of structure and content. You will find it on the CD or on your network. It lets you practise planning and producing multimedia products. Then, just like the SPB, you will showcase what you have done and how you did it in an eportfolio.

The final page in each chapter is called **Tackling THE PROJECT**. This will guide you through each stage of completing **THE PROJECT**.

Good luck and enjoy the course!

1 Investigating multimedia products

Multimedia plays an increasingly important part in our lives. It gives us access to information and knowledge in new and inspiring ways, using combinations of multimedia assets such as video, audio, animation, images and text.

When you log on to websites, play computer games, visit museums or go to modern shopping centres, you will almost certainly be seeing multimedia in action. You also encounter it every time you watch a DVD, use e-learning materials or, for that matter, the digimodules provided with this course.

In this chapter you will investigate a broad cross-section of multimedia products. You should make a real effort to investigate and evaluate as many products as you can, and do it in a focused way. Don't be fooled by technical wizardry – it may not really add anything to the product. Hopefully you will be inspired to develop your own products.

In this chapter you will learn about:

▶ *multimedia – what it is and what it is for*
▶ *the use of multimedia for a range of purposes*
▶ *the components of multimedia products*
▶ *how information in multimedia products is structured*
▶ *how to evaluate multimedia products effectively*

Why use multimedia?

A multimedia product is a combination of different components or assets that gives the user a multi-sensory experience. Websites and computer games are just two examples. They make use of video, audio, images and animation as well as text. If you intend to use only text in a product, you should think about writing a book or a report instead!

Multimedia can allow you to reach a bigger audience and to engage with people in a different way from books or newspapers.

How many different types of multimedia asset does this website use?

▶ It can be entertaining and exciting. Compare a traditional board game with its computer version.
▶ Movies and animations add excitement to learning. Imagine this book without its on-screen activities.
▶ Simulations can develop high-level skills such as flying an aircraft.
▶ Multimedia provides accessibility for people with disabilities by providing information in a number of formats.
▶ Multimedia can allow communication with a wider audience even if they speak a different language.

An example of a board game that can be played online

TALKING POINT 1.1

How many examples of multimedia products can you think of? What is the purpose of each one? Is the multimedia necessary or would the product be just as good without it?

Multimedia products are used widely in:

▶ education
▶ virtual reality
▶ entertainment and leisure.

Businesses and commercial organisations also use multimedia to promote their products and services.

Look at this company multimedia website

TALKING POINT 1.2

Banks, large stores, entertainment venues and airports are good places to see multimedia in action. Discuss the different ways in which multimedia is used in each of these locations.

The multimedia experience

Multimedia in education

One of the editors of this book can remember using a slate and chalk at school! The authors had only pen and paper, but you have so much more. Multimedia makes learning easier and more fun, through interactive materials, digital narratives or stories, and movies.

This ActiveBook is an example of an e-learning product that makes full use of different types of multimedia.

TALKING POINT 1.3

List the different ways in which multimedia is changing the way people learn. For example, how do young children benefit from interactive stories and talking books?

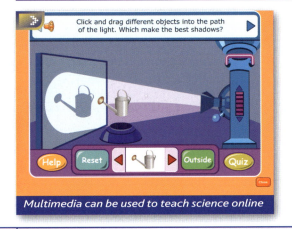

Multimedia can be used to teach science online

An interactive storybook for young children

▶▶ Activity 1.1

Look at some of the stories in the digital story section on the BBC website. Some are educational and others are for leisure.

How effective are these stories in conveying a message? How do the storytellers use still images to get a message across even when it includes action?

Encyclopedias

Online encyclopedias have many advantages compared with paper-based versions (or even CDs). Wikipedia is a good example. It has easy-to-follow hyperlinks that let you find out what you want to know and more besides. The pages are easy to read with lots of links and pictures. It can be updated on a daily basis to take account of things that are happening right now.

▶▶ Activity 1.2

Visit Wikipedia or another online encyclopedia and research a topic you are interested in. Make notes about the way in which multimedia enhances your experience. Share your findings with the rest of your group.

Quizzes

Multimedia quizzes can test so much more than a text-based quiz. The user can be asked to view pictures and videos and to listen to sound.

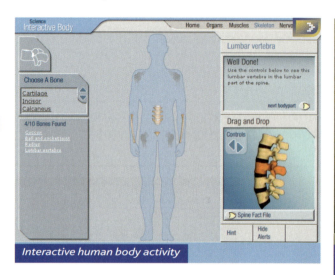

Interactive human body activity

Can you learn the social reactions needed to survive in a troop of chimps?

Museums

Modern museums have 'hands on' exhibits. These vary from interactive quizzes using touch-screen displays to complete simulations that surround you in a 'virtual reality' experience.

Museums often have websites with lots of extra information. The websites help you plan your day before you visit, or feature interactive activities that help you learn more about the things you have seen. A good example is the award-winning Conservation Central from the Smithsonian National Zoological Park in the United States.

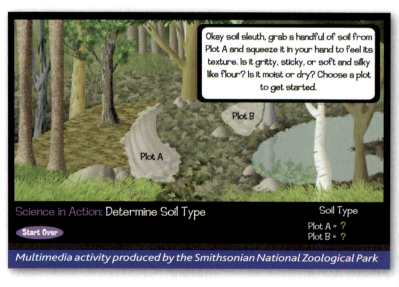

Multimedia activity produced by the Smithsonian National Zoological Park

Interactive display at The Deep submarium in Hull

Virtual reality

Simulations

Multimedia is used to simulate how things happen, to allow people to practise new techniques and to see how something might look.

In medicine, multimedia simulations can show how the body works in ways that would not be possible in a book. Other multimedia products allow doctors and medical students to practise procedures without endangering real patients and at a relatively low cost.

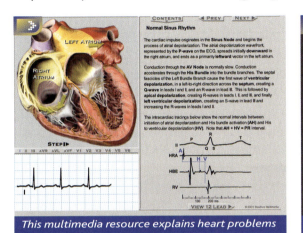

This multimedia resource explains heart problems

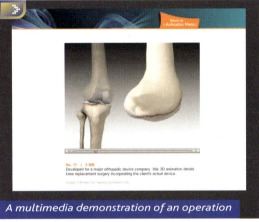

A multimedia demonstration of an operation

TALKING POINT 1.4

Multimedia simulations are sometimes used to train people to do things where there is an element of risk if things go wrong, or that would need lots of expensive equipment. Try to think of some examples.

Virtual tours

Estate agents use multimedia to provide virtual reality tours of houses. These let you 'walk through' all the rooms interactively and view the interiors from different angles.

▶▶ Activity 1.3

Investigate other uses for virtual tours, for example hotels and theme parks. Look at these websites to get you started.

Multimedia in entertainment and leisure

Multimedia and the arts

Many artists and musicians use multimedia to showcase their work and make it available to a wider audience.

▶▶ Activity 1.4

Visit the ART21 and Tate websites to see how multimedia is used to display the exhibits.

Computer games

Computer games are popular multimedia products. They can be anything from 'shoot 'em up' games or driving simulations to adventures in virtual worlds, such as Myst.

Multimedia games often feature the latest technology as manufacturers have to invest heavily in development to maintain sales. You can find games online and on CD and DVD, as well as games designed specifically for games consoles such as the Sony PS2.

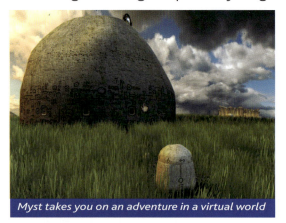

Myst takes you on an adventure in a virtual world

Some games can be played online

TALKING POINT 1.5

Choose some computer games and discuss how effective the use of multimedia is.

Multimedia devices

Multimedia is also now commonly found in everyday devices such as mobile phones and MP3 and DVD players. Many people like to be able to carry their media and information around with them and 'portability' is becoming increasingly important.

The new iPod
15,000 songs.
25,000 photos.
150 hours of video.

Multimedia on the move! Music, photos and video combined in one compact portable device

Features of a multimedia product

As you will have discovered by now, this ActiveBook uses different types of multimedia including video, audio, text, animation and images. How did the authors decide which types to use? What should you consider when designing your own products?

Video

Video is good for:

► showing action
► taking you to different locations
► helping you to visualise a story or event.

Video is less suitable for:

► scenes where there is little or no movement
► scenes where the action is very quick and hard to capture.

►► Activity 1.5

Watch this video clip. Try to decide why video was used rather than text or audio. How well do you think it works?

Audio

Audio is used extensively in multimedia products. Interviews, digital narratives and stories, commentaries and music are some examples. Can you think of any more?

TALKING POINT 1.6

It is often said that sound is more important than video in a multimedia product. Do you think that this is always true?

Images

Still images, such as photographs, are great for websites, video, presentations and simulations. They can be good for:

► getting across a message or telling a story, especially if the message has a strong emotional content
► creating a particular mood or atmosphere
► highlighting key points.

Still images can be linked together to create a movie. This technique is often used by writers of documentaries, and you will find it very useful.

What effect does the image on this web page have?

Animation

Interactive or animated graphics are often used on websites. They can be really useful and informative, especially if you want to explain a complicated idea or show how something works.

▶▶ Activity 1.6

These websites both use animations to explain complicated ideas. Select one of them and explain how the animation helps the user understand the idea. Think about how it would be explained without the animation.

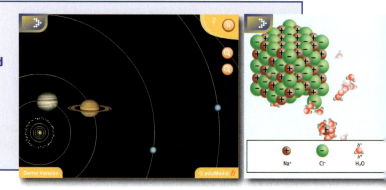

Text

Despite all that has been said above, text should not be ignored. Text is often the most effective way of setting the scene. Used in combination with other types of media, it can be a powerful way of describing a process.

▶▶ Activity 1.7

Look on the internet for examples of text being used effectively to get a message across. Compare your findings with others in the group.

Interactivity

When you watch a feature film, you need to watch it from the beginning to the end. If you were to watch the scenes jumbled up it wouldn't make sense. In many computer games you decide what happens next. This is an example of interactivity.

The pages or screens in a multimedia product can be organised in different ways:

- ▶ **Linear** – requires the user to view pages/screens in a pre-set order.
- ▶ **Hierarchical** – provides a number of different paths for the user to choose from.
- ▶ **Cluster** – provides most flexibility by allowing the user to move freely between all the pages/screens.

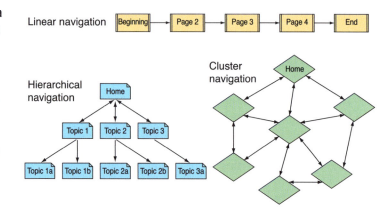

▶▶ Activity 1.8

Visit the BBC website and compare the navigation with this ActiveBook. Can you say what type of interactivity each product has? Does it depend on where you are in the product?

Other features of a multimedia product

Colour

There is no doubt that colour is an essential ingredient in an effective multimedia product. It can be used to:

- ► group similar items together
- ► draw attention
- ► emphasise important information
- ► enhance the user experience and create the right impression.

Even white space plays an important part in the design of a screen.

TALKING POINT 1.7

Find different examples of the use of colour and white space for different purposes in this ActiveBook. Use the list above to help you.

Navigation

If a product is interactive, the user must be able to move around it easily. Navigational aids such as buttons and links are an important feature of multimedia products.

TALKING POINT 1.8

Discuss the effectiveness of the navigational aids in this ActiveBook. Consider how they look on screen, whether their purpose is clear, and what you might do to improve them.

Multimedia around you

There is no doubt that you are surrounded by multimedia. Many multimedia products are designed for more than one audience. This is often done by using different multimedia assets for different screens.

You need to evaluate carefully what works and what does not. When looking at products, keep asking yourself:

- ► What is it for?
- ► Who is the product aimed at? Does it target more than one audience?
- ► Is it really suitable for its target audience(s)? Is it fit for purpose?
- ► Does the multimedia enhance the audience's experience or does it detract from it?
- ► Which types of multimedia have been used?
- ► How effective is the multimedia?
- ► What other features have been used?
- ► What type of interactivity does it have? Is it the right choice for the product?

Multimedia resources aimed at a variety of users

▸▸ Activity 1.9

Look at some multimedia products and try to answer the questions above.

Tackling THE PROJECT

THE PROJECT is similar to a real Unit 2 SPB but there are three main differences:

- ► You will work on sections of THE PROJECT as you complete each chapter. For the real SPB you will have at least 30 hours to do the whole project in one go.
- ► You don't have to produce a complete project plan for THE PROJECT because you are told when to tackle each section.
- ► There are more products in THE PROJECT than in the real SPB.

Open THE PROJECT and read each of the pages to make sure that you understand what you are being asked to do, especially the requirements for each product.

Look for good examples of the types of product you must produce for THE PROJECT.

Use a copy of this evaluation table to assess each product that you find. Save the tables in your user area. Could you use any of these features to help you achieve what you have been asked to produce?

Product:	Name:
Author:	Source:
Criteria	**Notes**
Target audience One or more?	
Purpose What is it for?	
Interactivity What type is it? Do all the buttons work? Does what you expect happen when you click a button or follow a link?	
Navigation What aids are used? Can you easily find your way around?	
Content Does the product use the media in an effective way? Is there a good balance between text and other media, such as video or images?	

Start to list your ideas either on paper or using mind-mapping software. This will help you when you come to the design stages. Save this list in your user area.

Create a directory folder

At this point you should create a directory folder structure so that you can organise files as you create them. This will make it easier to find them when you need them. You will require some, but not all, of these files for your eportfolio. You should be thinking about the structure and content of your eportfolio from the outset.

When I said you should investigate multimedia products, I didn't mean you to play computer games all night!

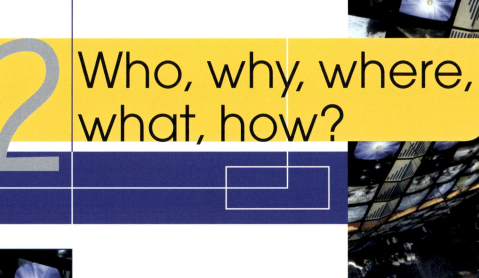

2 Who, why, where, what, how?

Filled with excitement by the potential of multimedia products, you may be tempted to launch into action and immediately start work on producing one of your own. This would be a mistake. You already know from your work in Unit 1 how important it is to establish requirements before you start.

The multimedia products you produce will be far more successful if you do some groundwork before starting to design and develop. First you must work out who the product is for, why it is needed, where it will be used and what must go in it. This is always the first phase in developing any product.

Other people have good ideas and you can make use of them to help you be creative. You should investigate similar products before you start on your designs.

Before you progress further you need to make sure that you are on the right track by asking other people what they think of your ideas. You need to present your ideas clearly if the feedback is to be useful. You must find suitable people to ask for feedback and then decide what changes you need to make, if any.

In this chapter you will learn how to investigate requirements and produce initial designs for multimedia products by deciding:

▶ *who the target audience is*
▶ *why the product is needed*
▶ *where it is for*
▶ *what must go in it*
▶ *how to present ideas*
▶ *how to gather and make use of feedback*

The Deep

Scenario

The Deep is the world's only submarium. It is based in Hull in Yorkshire. It traces the evolution of our planet since the start of time and looks at how life in the world's oceans has developed and changed. It contains one of the largest aquarium tanks in Europe. It houses many different species from around the world.

Pages from The Deep's website

The Deep needs more multimedia products to attract new visitors and to promote educational use of the facilities.

Web pages

A new section of the website will target teachers and students. It will include features to use both before and after they visit. The focus must be educational, but it must also be fun and entertaining.

Short movie

A multimedia trailer will be sent to schools and colleges as a free sample of what is on offer at The Deep.

Scrolling presentation

A presentation will run continuously on a large display screen in the foyer area at the front of The Deep. It will feature some of the main attractions.

The main audience for these new products is school students, but it is also hoped they will attract more visitors to The Deep.

Two focus group meetings have been organised, one for teachers and one for students. The purpose of these meetings is to ensure that the designers are on the right track. The feedback received will be used to develop the designs for the new products.

The foyer of The Deep

TALKING POINT 2.1

Why do you think The Deep has selected these three products? What other multimedia products would attract students like you?

▶▶ Activity 2.1

Staff at The Deep have already developed some resources for students and teachers to use when they visit the submarium. Visit the website and look at some of these. For each resource you look at, identify the audience and see how multimedia is used. Are the resources effective?

Who is it for?

The more you know about your target audience, the easier it will be to develop a product that meets their needs.

Some of the resources developed by The Deep

TALKING POINT 2.2

What do you need to find out about a target audience before you can make progress with your designs for a product?

There are many ways of gathering information about a target audience. The Deep uses focus groups – this involves organising meetings with appropriate people who represent the intended audience.

TALKING POINT 2.3

Listen to the recordings of The Deep's focus group meetings. The students and teachers are talking about the new area of the website.

Record your thoughts about what the teachers and students would like to see. You might like to use a Venn diagram to organise your ideas.

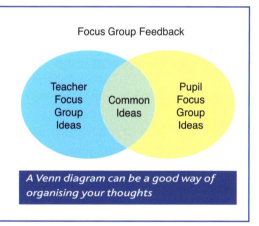

Focus Group Feedback

A Venn diagram can be a good way of organising your thoughts

▶▶ Activity 2.2

You need to establish the requirements for each of the products for THE PROJECT. The first stage is to find out as much as possible about the audience for each one.

Produce a mind map or similar diagram for each product to record everything you know about the target audience.

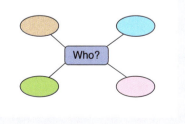

Why is it needed?

Establishing the exact purpose of a multimedia product is not always as simple as it sounds. A product may have more than one purpose.

For example, The Deep wants the new products to attract more visitors. This is a clear central purpose, but what does it actually mean? Do they just want more people through the entrance each day? Do they want more people of particular ages? Are there days of the week that have lower numbers and could take more visitors? Do they need to attract more people in the local area or are they hoping to persuade those living further afield to make the journey to visit?

Do you want to entertain?

If the main purpose of a multimedia product is to entertain the audience, the product must be fun to use and something that people might choose to use in their leisure time. You may well have some choice in the content.

Do you want to educate?

If so, what do you want the audience to learn? How can you use multimedia to make the learning more effective? How can you check that the product has done its job?

Do you want to inform?

If you need to convey particular information, you must ensure that the multimedia you use helps to get the message across without distracting the audience. It is, of course, essential to check that the information is accurate.

Do you want to sell?

If the main purpose of the product is to sell something, it must attract attention, provide accurate information and, most importantly, make people want to buy it.

Is it single or multi-purpose?

A product will often have more than one purpose. For example, a multimedia game may be entertaining, but its main purpose may be educational. Look out for 'hidden' purposes.

The interactive zone at The Deep

TALKING POINT 2.4

For each product for The Deep, identify its main purpose using the above list to help you. Do the products have any other purposes?

▸▸ Activity 2.3

Make sure that you are clear about the purpose(s) for each of the products for THE PROJECT. Keep a record of this information either in note form or as a mind map.

Where is it for?

It is important that you establish exactly where a product will be used before you start to design it. Understanding the characteristics of a location is crucial if you are going to design a product that will work in that environment. Factors you need to consider include:

Venue and position

Is the product going to be one of many things competing for users' attention or is it the focal point? Is it indoors or outdoors? How close can the user get to the screen?

Size and type of screen

Is the product to be projected onto a large screen or whiteboard? Or is it meant to be viewed on a computer monitor? What size will the screen be?

Level of background noise

Will sound work in this location? For example, there is no point in having a voiceover on a virtual tour if it is to be shown in a noisy exhibition hall.

Lighting

Can the lighting be adjusted to ensure that the display is clear? If not, this will affect your choice of colour combinations and contrast.

User involvement and assistance

Will users be able to view the product in passing or will they need to interact with it? Will they need to use it without help or will someone be there to assist them?

TALKING POINT 2.5

Look at each of these photographs, taken at The Deep. What can you tell about the location in each case? What else would you need to know before designing a product for this location?

▶▶ Activity 2.4

For each of the products for THE PROJECT, make sure you are clear where it is to be used. What effect does the location have on the content you should include and the way you present it?

What must go in it?

If you know who a product is for, why it is needed and where it is to be used, you can start to think about what must go in it. A product will have two types of content:

- ▶ **Necessary information** – this is what the audience must know and is often specified in a project brief. For example, contact details or copyright information.
- ▶ **Other content to help get a message across** – this is where you can be creative. For example, you might decide that a movie clip or an image will help to convey the information.

First make sure that you are clear about what is required and then think about what else you need to include. There are several techniques you can use to help you.

Brainstorming

Brainstorming is a process for generating ideas quickly, without stopping to worry about whether the ideas are good.

Brainstorming involves a group of people coming up with as many ideas as they can very quickly. One person starts off with an idea, then other people in the group join in, saying what immediately comes into their minds. Many of these ideas will be useless, but that doesn't matter. People continue to shout out ideas until they dry up or start to repeat old ones.

You can use a whiteboard, a piece of paper, a flipchart or even sticky labels stuck to a wall to record the ideas. It is important that everybody can see them clearly as this helps generate new ideas.

The Deep's designers had a brainstorming session to come up with ideas for multimedia products. Here are their notes.

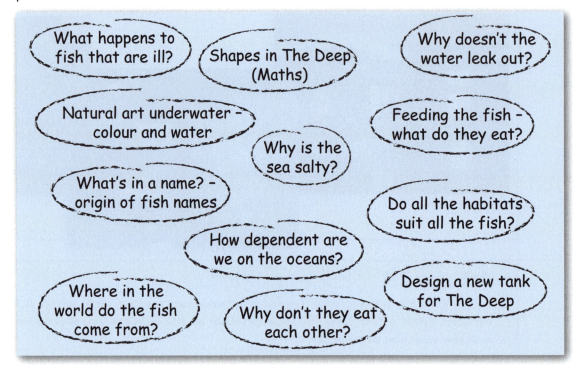

What happens to fish that are ill?

Shapes in The Deep (Maths)

Why doesn't the water leak out?

Natural art underwater – colour and water

Why is the sea salty?

Feeding the fish – what do they eat?

What's in a name? – origin of fish names

Do all the habitats suit all the fish?

How dependent are we on the oceans?

Where in the world do the fish come from?

Why don't they eat each other?

Design a new tank for The Deep

Mind-mapping

Mind-mapping software can be used to record brainstorming discussions visually as they occur. However, it is more often used to organise the ideas later when symbols and pictures can be added.

Look at this example of a mind map, created by The Deep's designers using mind-mapping software to present their ideas. It shows their initial ideas for the web pages for The Deep. Work in groups and use mind maps or diagrams to decide what you think should go into the other two products.

▶▶ Activity 2.5

For each of the products for THE PROJECT, produce a mind map or similar diagram to show what must go in it. Then add all the other content and features that you think would help make the products fit for purpose.

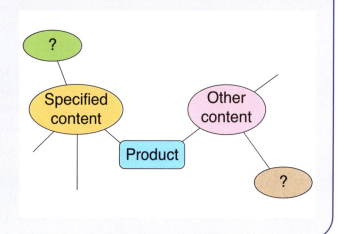

Now is the time to pull together all the information you have gathered about THE PROJECT. Work as a group to produce a complete picture of what is required. If you are using mind-mapping software, you might want to create one large diagram. For each product, include as much information as you can about:

▶ *who it is for*
▶ *why it is needed*
▶ *where it will be used*
▶ *what information must go in it.*

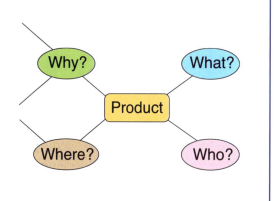

Generating ideas

Researching the topic

Most products focus on a particular topic or area of interest. For example, **THE PROJECT** is about recycling. It is important to spend time gathering information about the topic before you decide what to include in a product. Where you look for this information will depend on the topic.

TALKING POINT 2.8

You have been asked to provide information on aspects of recycling in the products for **THE PROJECT**. *Where should you look for information to go into each of the products?*

▸▸ Activity 2.6

Spend some time researching recycling for THE PROJECT. There are lots of sources of information you could use. Your local council's website might be a good place to start.

Make notes as you go along. Do *not* be tempted to simply copy and paste text from websites. Remember to keep a record of the sources you find so that you can refer back to them and they can be acknowledged.

Sources of inspiration

How often have you thought of a good idea only to find that someone else got there first? Very few ideas are truly original. You must not steal other people's ideas, but you can use them as sources of inspiration to give you ideas.

In Chapter 1 you investigated a number of different multimedia products. Some of these were similar to those you will need to produce for **THE PROJECT**. You looked at how different types of multimedia had been used and evaluated how effective they were.

▸▸ Activity 2.7

Look back at the evaluation tables you produced for THE PROJECT in Chapter 1. Revisit the products you looked at and note down ideas for features and techniques you could include in your own products. Add these to the list you started in Chapter 1.

Eliminating ideas

Once you have a list of ideas, you need to take a close look at them. Remind yourself of who, why, where and what and then remove ideas that are not suitable. Here are some possible reasons why you might reject ideas:

- ▶ the idea is not appropriate for the target audience
- ▶ the idea does not relate to the purpose of the product
- ▶ there is not enough time to turn the idea into reality
- ▶ you don't have the equipment to produce it
- ▶ you don't have the necessary skills to produce it.

TALKING POINT 2.9

Look closely at the table below. This shows the reasons why some ideas for the web pages were rejected by The Deep. Can you see why they rejected each one? What are they taking into account when making each decision?

Initial ideas	Reason for rejection
How do you keep the water from leaking out?	Young children are often interested by this question, but the answer may be difficult for them to understand. It is difficult to see how it would be shown in an interesting way on the website.
What's in a name – the origins of fish names	This is another interesting topic with the fish having common names as well as Latin ones. But it would be hard for young children to understand and it does not link in very well with the primary school curriculum.
How do you create the ideal habitat for all the fish?	This requires the children to have considerable scientific understanding and may be too difficult for them. It would also be very difficult to show through multimedia.
Where in the world do all the fish come from? Have you been there on holiday? FINDING NEMO Game (help get Nemo back home)	This is a great topic for teaching geography. Students could plot the fish on a map of the world with hotspots giving more details etc. However, it may be hard or impossible to get permission to use the Finding Nemo brand.
Natural art – underwater colours	It might be difficult to show the true colours of an aquarium on a computer screen because of variation in the way monitors are set up.
How do you look after a fish that is ill?	This may lead to bad publicity for The Deep and may not be what they are looking for.
Why is the sea salty?	How would we show this process on screen? Possibly by using Flash animations, but these might be expensive to produce.
What and how do you feed the fish?	This is an interesting topic but it's similar to some of the others (for example, why don't they eat each other?).

▶▶ Activity 2.8

Use the same approach to go through your own ideas for THE PROJECT.
Consider whether each one is appropriate. Revise and re-save your list.

Getting feedback on your ideas

Once you have created a list of ideas and eliminated the impractical ones, you are ready to present your ideas to others for feedback.

For the new web pages for The Deep, the designers narrowed the choice down to three ideas:

- ▶ Design your own tank (Design and technology)
- ▶ Which part of the world do the fish come from? (Geography)
- ▶ Shapes in The Deep (Maths).

They wrote a brief description of each of the ideas so that they could get some feedback on them.

TALKING POINT 2.10

Read the description of each idea. What do you think of each one? Which do you think will work best? Remind yourself of the audience and purpose before deciding.

Prototype 1 – Design your own tank

This is an idea based around an existing teaching resource on The Deep's website. In the original activity, pupils plan out on paper a new tank display for the Deep, taking into account the space and size available. Then they suggest fish the tank and complete a costing exercise to make sure they could do it within budget.

Our proposal takes this on a step further by using multimedia. Pupils could use drag and drop functionality (built using Flash) to lay out their new tank within a given space. The idea would be based around a competition to design the best tank within a given budget. After designing the layout of the tank pupils would design the interior of the tank. This would involve research on the internet to find out what conditions different species like to live in. Finally they would use a live spreadsheet to calculate how many different fish they could purchase for £25,000.

Prototype 2 – Where in the world do these fish come from?

This is a new exercise designed to help students get a better idea of the geography of the world. In particular, it is hoped students will get a better idea of the different oceans in which fish live.

The activities will be based around the film 'Finding Nemo' – the idea being to help Nemo's father find Nemo. On his many journeys he comes across lots of different species of fish and learns where in the world they live. It would take the form of a game that involves locating fish on a map of the world and matching them to the oceans they live in.

Prototype 3 – Shapes in The Deep

This is a maths exercise based on the many geometric shapes which appear as part of The Deep itself. Pupils will be able to undertake many mathematical exercises such as measuring and predicating angles, working out surface areas and identifying different shapes.

The activity will be based on a computer model of The Deep that students will be able to move on screen in order to measure the angles and undertake the maths projects.

To be sure you are on the right track, you need to give people a clear picture of what you have in mind. In addition to the topics, you should give an indication of colour schemes, number of pages/screens, features to be included and how multimedia will be used.

Presenting ideas

You could produce a written description like those produced by The Deep's designers, but there are many other ways of presenting your ideas:

Thumbnail sketches – to give a rough idea of what something might look like.

Outline storyboards – to indicate what will appear on key pages/screens and how they might link together.

Examples of similar products – to give the user a feel for how your final product will look and feel.

Samples of similar uses of multimedia and other features – to show what you are thinking of using in your products.

Making use of feedback

Gathering feedback

No matter how many times you check what you have done, there will always be things to improve. If your product is to stand any chance of being fit for purpose, you must ensure that you get reliable feedback from the right people at every stage.

If you choose people who are representative of your target audience, you are more likely to get useful feedback on your ideas. However, you must make sure that they clearly understand who the product is for, why it is needed, where it will be used and what must go in it so that they can make valid judgements.

Take this opportunity to gather feedback on all the possibilities you are considering, including those you are not sure about.

At this stage, your ideas are very sketchy so don't expect your test users to look at them on their own — make sure that you are available to answer queries and give extra information.

Don't forget to record all the feedback you receive, however trivial it seems. It will help you in the next stage of the process, particularly if you organise it logically.

Using feedback

There is no point in getting feedback if you don't make use of it. However, you may not agree with all the feedback and you do not have to take it all on board. If you decide to disregard a comment, it is always worth recording your reason for future reference.

When you are exploring ideas you need to make sure that what you are considering is suitable for the target audience. Don't be distracted by things you like or things you enjoy producing. Students often spend far too long trying to include all sorts of fancy features in a product just because they are fun, when they should be concentrating on things that the audience actually needs.

TALKING POINT 2.11

Listen to the feedback the designers received about their ideas and make notes. Does the feedback make you think differently about which of the three ideas the designers should take forward?

The designers at The Deep listened carefully to the feedback they received on the three final ideas. They changed their initial suggestions to take account of this feedback where they agreed with it.

▸▸ Activity 2.9

You should by now have a clear idea of who, why, where and what for each of the products in THE PROJECT. Take time to make sure that you have all the information you need.

Tackling THE PROJECT

P

Now it is time to tackle the 'Investigating Requirements' section of THE PROJECT.

Checkpoint!

By now you should be clear about the audience and purpose of each of the products, where they will be used and what content is required. You should also have used techniques like brainstorming and mind-mapping to generate your initial thoughts.

You should have found some sources of inspiration and compiled a list of ideas for the products.

Now it is time to firm up your ideas. These need to be detailed enough to share with others so that they can give you useful feedback. You have a lot to think about — as well as the information itself you must decide how to make best use of multimedia tools to present it.

Presenting your ideas

Decide how you are going to present your ideas for feedback. Will you work on paper or use software tools? Remember that anything you want to include in your eportfolio must eventually be saved in an acceptable digital format. Make sure that you include all the information a test user needs to be able to make sensible comments.

Making use of feedback

Ask suitable people for comments and record their feedback so that you can take account of it in your final designs.

Save a record of your initial ideas, the feedback you receive and notes on how you intend to use it. You will need all this material for use in your eportfolio, particularly in commentaries and the project review. Remember to use sensible file names so that you can find things again.

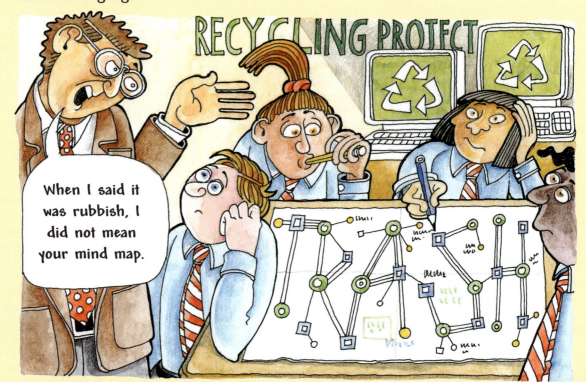

3 Multimedia design

Once you have firmed up your initial design ideas for a multimedia product, the next stage is to produce detailed designs.

Look at your initial designs for **THE PROJECT**. Would somebody else be able to build the products using your notes? Probably not! Even though you are going to build them yourself, you still need to have far more detailed designs before you start.

Suppose the designers at The Deep wanted to produce a video about life on the ocean floor. To do this they might need to hire special underwater cameras and employ a diver for the day. This is expensive, so it's essential that they get all the shots they need and that they don't have to organise another shoot. How would they do this? Detailed design is the answer.

Producing multimedia products can be time-consuming and expensive. It's important to get things as near right as possible at the first attempt.

In this chapter you will learn how to design multimedia products by:

► *deciding what assets you need and where to get them from*
► *creating an assets library*
► *using structure charts, storyboards, timelines and flowcharts*
► *getting feedback on your designs*
► *taking account of the feedback you receive*

Why waste time on detailed design?

If you have a good idea of what you want to produce, why not simply get stuck in and create the product?

- ► Multimedia products are complicated and there are lots of components that have to work together. All pathways must be correct and links must go to the right places.
- ► You must gather everything you need for a product before you can create it. How will you know what you need if you don't have a detailed design?
- ► You must be sure that it is a quality product with the right colours, fonts, style and layout.
- ► You must be able to communicate your intentions so that you can get good feedback.

Assets

Imagine you are going to bake a chocolate cake. You need a recipe and you need to make sure you have all the ingredients together before you start. The recipe for a multimedia product is your detailed design. The ingredients are your assets. Each asset is a multimedia component such as an image, a movie clip, text or a button. Once you have them all you can start 'mixing' them to build your final product, using your design as the recipe.

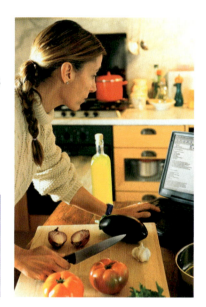

TALKING POINT 3.1

Think of all the reasons why you should be careful to identify and gather all the assets you need before you start to build a product. What do you think will happen if you start building a product only to find that you don't have all the assets you need?

Sources

You must make sure that it is possible to find or create each asset before you include it in your design.

You should be able to find some ready-made assets, such as images from picture galleries or clips from film libraries. You must be aware of copyright issues when sourcing materials from secondary sources. You should check that you can use an asset at this stage. There is no point in including an asset in your design only to find at the building stage that you haven't got permission to use it. If in doubt, leave it out!

You will need to produce some of the assets yourself. Allow plenty of time for this.

Don't be tempted to start building a product until you have all the assets you need. You will probably need to spend time editing those you have gathered from secondary sources as well as creating your own.

Using an assets library

As you gather assets, you can start to build a library. As you will discover, preparing assets is a time-consuming process so you will want to reuse assets wherever you can. You will need to organise your library of assets so that you can easily find things when you need them. There is more on this in Chapter 4.

If you are producing more than one product with a common theme, it makes sense to use some of the same assets in the different products. This reinforces the relationship between the products. A logo is an example of an asset often used for this purpose.

Where are the assets?

As you start designing your products you need to think about where you might get the assets from. It is essential that you know exactly what is needed so that you stay on track. We all know how easy it is to get distracted when searching for something on the internet!

There are some important points to bear in mind when deciding whether you can rely on secondary sources or whether you need to create your own assets using primary sources.

Still images

We live in a very visual world – it is often said that 'a picture is worth a thousand words'. Look around you at how images are used in books, posters, magazines, packaging and logos. They are all competing for your attention. Here are just a few of the ways you can use images in multimedia products:

▶ photos and drawings for illustration
▶ icons and buttons for navigation and control
▶ maps or diagrams to explain something
▶ logos
▶ textures to provide interesting backgrounds for your slides or screens.

When using still images in a multimedia product you need to be aware that:

▶ they often need to be compressed and this can affect the quality
▶ you must make sure you have permission to use them
▶ they should complement other content and not just be used for their own sake.

Still images can be more effective than moving images (video). Your audience can focus on a still image without being distracted by movement. However, there is software that allows you to 'move' around a still image to give the impression of movement. You can also link still images together in a sequence.

Stills can have a dramatic impact

Video

If a picture is worth a thousand words, is a moving image worth more? Used well, moving images can make you feel as if you are part of the action. They can also explain subjects in ways that would be difficult or impossible with text or images alone.

TALKING POINT 3.2

Think about situations where video would be an essential asset. Can you think of any drawbacks in using video?

If you decide to include video in a product, you generally need to keep it short. You can always split longer video clips into shorter clips. If you need to compress your video to reduce the size this may affect the quality.

▶▶ **Activity 3.1**

Look at these compressed video clips in your ActiveBook. Which types work well and which do not?

Scene with lots of dialogue   *Landscape shots*   *Fast action scenes*

TALKING POINT 3.3

Watch a couple of news reports on TV or on the internet. Identify the different ways in which video is used. How effective are they?

Audio

Audio adds an extra dimension to multimedia products. Most computers let you record sound digitally directly to the hard disk and then edit or manipulate it.

You might use audio to add:

▶ a commentary or voiceover to a movie or digital narrative
▶ music to a movie
▶ sound effects to reflect something happening on screen.

Think carefully before you use music. Many people add music which they do not have permission to use. There are lots of copyright restrictions on the use of commercial music, even for educational purposes, so you must have a good reason for using it. It must serve a purpose, for example to create emotional impact. Don't include music just because it is your favourite track or group.

▶▶ **Activity 3.2**

Some websites allow you to use copyright music for free in your own products. Have a close look at what each of these websites offer and the terms of any licences that apply.

Freeplay Music   Magnatune   Opsound

Animation

Animated diagrams are ideal for explaining how things happen or work. Animated maps can bring geography to life. As with most multimedia assets, you must be careful not to use animations for their own sake. If you include an animation, be sure that you can justify its use.

Text

It is harder to read text on a screen than on a printed page. People tend to skim over it rather than read all the details. Try to limit your use of text to occasions when you cannot convey the message with other forms of media.

If you need to use text, present it in short, easy-to-read chunks. It must grab the audience's attention and keep it. Use crisp, clear words that suit the subject and keep your audience interested. Choose your fonts carefully. Most people find sans serif fonts easier to read than serif fonts.

Using design tools

There are a number of different design tools you can use to produce your final designs. In this section we will follow the progress of The Deep's designers as they start producing designs for their multimedia products. You can use similar tools to help you design many different multimedia products.

Structure charts

A structure chart is like a bird's-eye view of a product. It gives an overview of how a product is organised and how different parts link to each other. Structure charts can be used to show the structure of multimedia products such as websites, games and simulations.

The Deep's designers used a structure chart to show the organisation of the new section of the website.

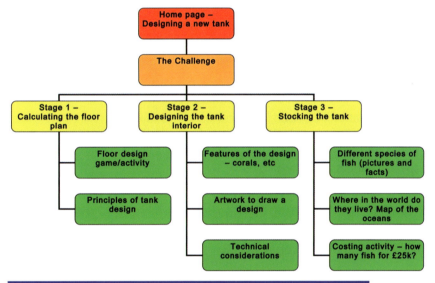

Part of the structure chart for the new section of The Deep's website

Notice how the structure chart shows four levels of pages for the website:

Home page – this is the page that users see first when they enter this section of the website.
Challenge page – this introduces the three main stages and allows users to select any one.
Stage pages – one for each stage.
Activity pages – two or more for each stage.

TALKING POINT 3.4

Structure charts don't tell you everything you need to know in order to build a multimedia product. What can you work out about The Deep's plans for the new section of the website just by looking at the structure chart? What else would you need to know before you could build the product?

▸▸ Activity 3.3

Create a structure chart for your information point for THE PROJECT.

Storyboards

Storyboards are used to map out the visual layout of screens in a product. They can be used to design the screens for products such as information points, presentations and websites.

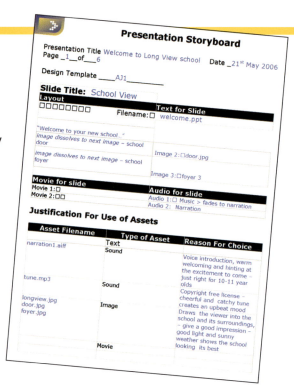

A storyboard must include:

- ► a representation of what will be seen, both content and layout
- ► notes about colour, size, font, resolution, logos, titles
- ► notes about audio and narration
- ► notes about special effects and transitions.

A storyboard need only be a rough sketch. It does not have to be a work of art, but it does need to contain enough detail to communicate the complete screen design to others. If it does not, you won't be able to get good feedback.

You must decide what assets you need and make sure that you achieve a multi-sensory experience by:

- ► selecting the most appropriate types
- ► having a balance of different types.

Producing a storyboard

There is nothing wrong with sketching storyboards on paper – many people prefer this method, including the designers at The Deep (see pages 34–35). However, you need to remember that when it comes to the SPB any paper-based evidence you want to include will need to be scanned in. Alternatively, you can use any suitable software. This example was produced using the drawing tools that come with a word processing package.

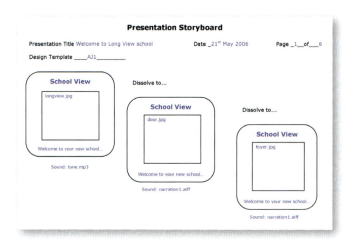

Presentation software is another option. Look at this example. Notice how it includes images alongside the text.

Discuss the pros and cons of different methods of producing storyboards.

▸▸Activity 3.4

Use any suitable method to produce a storyboard for your information point for The Project. Check your structure chart to ensure that you include the correct links.

Templates

It is important to keep the overall design of products such as presentations and websites consistent. Templates help you do this.

Which features of web pages need to be consistent? How does a template help to do this? Look at The Deep's website to help you decide.

Flowcharts

A flowchart is used to show the paths through a product. A fully interactive product such as an information point will have many different routes through it. It should be possible to see all the alternative paths by looking at the flowchart.

These are the common symbols used in a flowchart. Arrows are used to show the direction of flow between them.

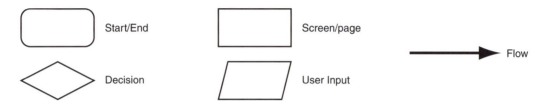

Symbol	Name
(rounded rectangle)	Start/End
(rectangle)	Screen/page
(arrow)	Flow
(diamond)	Decision
(parallelogram)	User Input

TALKING POINT 3.7

Look at this section of a flowchart for a simple quiz. What does it tell you about the paths a user can take?

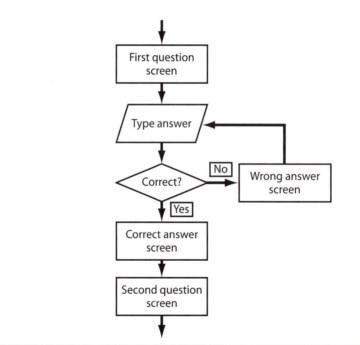

▸▸Activity 3.5

Create a flowchart for the quiz for THE PROJECT.

▸▸Activity 3.6

Give your flowchart to another member of the group and ask them to describe how the quiz works. What paths could a user take depending on the answers they give?

Designing a movie

A movie consists of a combination of text (written and spoken), audio and visual effects (images, video and animation). It runs for a fixed amount of time during which the content is constantly changing. A design for a movie must describe clearly what is happening on the screen at any one time.

Once you know what you want the movie to achieve, you can decide how long it should be and what scenes you want to include. The next step is to produce a timeline to show what would be happening on the screen at each point during the movie.

Look at the example of a timeline for a movie trailer on the next page. You can see that even a short movie uses a number of different multimedia assets. These need to be organised so that everything happens at the right time.

Layers

The layers of a timeline provide a way to organise the assets and show the transitions in a movie. They show where an asset is introduced, how long it lasts, and any transitions.

Content is put on different layers so that start and stop times can overlap. You can use as many layers as you like, but be careful not to make your movie too complex or busy. If you have too much going on at once, you will make the audience feel sick!

TALKING POINT 3.8

Study the example of a timeline overleaf. What does it tell you about the multimedia assets and their behaviour? Why are some of the file names missing? Can you describe what the viewer will experience during the movie?

▸▸ Activity 3.7

Use a timeline to design your movie trailer for THE PROJECT.

Designing a digital narrative

A digital narrative or story is a type of movie. It tells a story and can be interactive.

TALKING POINT 3.9

The example overleaf is about making a cake. Can you describe what the viewer will experience? The storyboard is incomplete — how would you complete the narrative?

The storyboard consists of a number of stages (screens) linked by transitions. There is a sketch for each stage indicating the position of assets on the screen, colours, sizes, etc. In the table there is a list of the assets associated with that stage and a description of the transitions that will take the screen to the next stage.

Transitions can include descriptions of animations, actions such as text appearing on the screen, sound track fading in and out or events triggered by the user.

The script for any voiceovers may be too long to include on the storyboard, in which case it can be stored as a separate document and referenced on the storyboard.

▸▸ Activity 3.8

Produce a narrative storyboard for your digital story for THE PROJECT.

TIMELINE FOR MOVIE – HIGHTOWN STADIUM

	0	5	10	15	20	25
Video/Image	Flag animation (flag.gif)		Night shot	Day shot	Video of players in warm-up	
Transition/effect			Wipe down	Dissolve		
Audio					Fade in music band.wav	Music plays
Narration		"Welcome to Hightown Stadium"				
Text		Title: Hightown Stadium				

STORYBOARD FOR DIGITAL NARRATIVE – MAKING A CHOCOLATE CAKE

 →  →

Stage 1	Transition	Stage 2	Transition
Images: Table Drawings of white mixing bowl and wooden spoon Clipart of scales (scales.jpg)	Bag of flour moves in from right at same time as butter moves up Then three eggs drop down one at a time at same time as bag of sugar moves in from right Clicking an ingredient triggers a text box with description/measurements.	**Images:** Table Drawings of white mixing bowl, wooden spoon and eggs Clipart of scales (scales.jpg) Photos of flour, sugar, butter, cocoa	Fade out scre Fade in mixin cake mixture wooden spoo Fade in seque of flour, oper smaller butte shells Clicking the triggers vide the ingredien
Audio: quiet music in the background			
Narration: Intro script	**Narration:** Ingredients script	**Narration:** Method script	
		Text boxes for ingredients	

30		35		40		45		50		55		60
				Player entrance shot		Aerial view (Stadium.jpg)				Flag animation (flag.gif)		
				Ease in then zoom in		Zoom out from players' entrance						
								Fade out music				

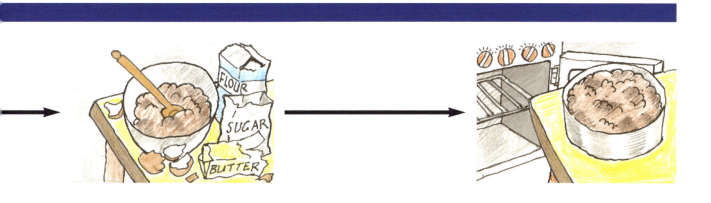

	Stage 3	Transition	Stage 4
	Images:		**Images:**
l with	Table		Open oven in background
e and	Mixing bowl with cake mixture visible and wooden spoon in it		Cake mixture in tin
			Table
open bag	Open bags of flour and sugar, smaller butter and egg shells		
f sugar,			
egg			
bowl			
e mixing			
	Video: Mixing ingredients Return to stage 3 screen when video finishes		

Feedback on designs

Before you go on to build a product you should check and re-check to make sure that the design is complete. It should have enough annotation for someone else to understand exactly what you have in mind. Complete designs should enable you to build a product that is fit for audience and purpose.

To be sure that your designs are good enough, you must show them to other people and get feedback. Some of these people should be representative of the target audience. As always, they need to be clear about who the product is for, why it is needed, where it will be used and what must go in it.

It is important to make good use of feedback throughout the design process. Remind yourself of what was said in Chapter 2 about how to use feedback. It is important to record the feedback and how you respond to it.

This table shows some of the feedback The Deep's designers received while they were working on the storyboard for the web pages. They used this feedback to help them complete their final designs.

Storyboard	Media to be included	Feedback received
A simple home page with a graphic of The Deep (left) and the principal activities (right)	▶ Image graphic (The Deep) ▶ Text describing different pages ▶ Image for buttons	What colours will you use? I think you should use Verdana font, it's easy to read. Delete 'HOME PAGE' and make 'DESIGN A NEW TANK' the title. Move image to the right and buttons to left so that text is to the right of each button.
The challenge page. It is intended that all users will start from here and select one of the four challenges below. Introduced with voiceover and video.	▶ Video clip (CEO talking) ▶ Images (four separate challenges) ▶ Text for each challenge	Not sure that this matches your structure chart. What are you doing about accessibility for the voiceover? Does the talking head start automatically?

Storyboard	Media to be included	Feedback received
Challenge 1: Floor layout of tank based on interactive game (Flash) and design principles.	▸ Interactive graphic (FLASH) for floor plan activity ▸ Audio recording – marine expert on tank design	What goes here? Need storyboard and transcript.
Challenge 2: The coral reef exercise. Find out about corals, how they grow and how they can be simulated in aquaria. Lots of audio clips of experts and video clips.	▸ Video clips (corals, coral manufacturer, etc.) ▸ Audio clips (expert speaking) ▸ Image – corals	What will the experts say? I can't see a transcript. Page is very busy, difficult to see what each box is for. Don't think this will appeal to schoolchildren.
Database exercise on fish, species and where in the world they come from. Links the fish to a map of the world's oceans (Flash based).	▸ Graphic for map of world's oceans ▸ Flash activity to link database to location on map ▸ Images of fish for database	Not sure how this is supposed to work. Do I choose a fish from the list and drag it to the ocean, or do I click on the ocean and the list changes to show the fish that live there? Screen is cluttered on left and title hard to see. Nice idea but screen looks boring.

TALKING POINT 3.10

What feedback would you give to the designers to help them improve their designs?

▸▸ Activity 3.9

Check your storyboard and structure chart for the information point for THE PROJECT. Give them to another member of your group and ask them to describe what the product will look like and how it will work. Is there enough detail? Would they be able to build the product using this information? Make a note of this feedback, which you will need later.

Tackling **THE PROJECT**

It's time to complete the detailed design for each of your products. You should already have made a start on this during the chapter.

You need to identify the complete set of design documents needed for each product. Check that you have everything in this list.

- ▶ **For your digital story:** a narrative storyboard with a timeline to show the stages and transitions between them.
- ▶ **For your movie:** a timeline with layers showing the sequence of events.
- ▶ **For your scrolling presentation:** a storyboard which details the content and layout for each slide and the transitions between them.
- ▶ **For your information point:** a structure chart to show the overall organisation and a storyboard for the screens.
- ▶ **For your quiz:** a structure chart to show the overall organisation; a flowchart to show the different paths available depending on which answer the user selects; and a storyboard for the screens.

Remember to think about the audience and purpose of each product. As you go along, make a list of the assets you need to gather. Don't forget that you can use an asset in more than one product. You may have to change an asset in some way to make it suitable, so make a note of any editing or reformatting that is needed.

As a guide to the level of detail that is required in your designs, ask yourself the following question:

Have I included enough detail for someone else to be able to produce what it was I had in mind?

If the answer is 'no', you need to add the missing information.

Don't include things for the sake of it. If a particular type of asset does not enhance the user experience, then don't include it.

Show your designs to someone else and ask them what they think of them. Keep a record of their comments. Where you think they have made valid suggestions, alter your designs accordingly.

Save your designs and notes on feedback in the appropriate folders.

4 Collecting and preparing assets

With detailed designs in place, you know what you want to produce and for whom. It's now time to get to grips with the practical aspects of preparing all the assets you need.

Preparing assets is a time-consuming process, so it makes sense to use existing material whenever you can. You can gather raw material from secondary sources such as image collections, film libraries and archives. But don't just assume that it's OK to use someone else's work. You must understand about copyright and stay within the law by making sure that you have permission before you use something.

It's unlikely that you will find all the assets you need from secondary sources, so be prepared to go out and create some material of your own. You will use a range of equipment to capture images, video and sound.

Multimedia editing tools will help you to prepare your assets. This process can be time-consuming, and sometimes you have to make difficult decisions about what to keep and what to get rid of. It's always a good idea to repurpose assets if you can by using them in different ways for different purposes. This saves time and can also provide a visual link between your products.

In this chapter you will learn how to collect and create multimedia assets by:

▶ *gathering them from suitable secondary sources*
▶ *creating them yourself*
▶ *editing and repurposing them*

Staying on the right side of the law

You will have looked at other people's ideas and work for sources of inspiration. Some of this material is available for you to use in your own products, but some is not. How do you know what you can use?

Copyright

If someone else has created an asset, you need their permission to use it. All material on the internet is subject to copyright unless it says it is not.

Most websites have a link called something like 'Terms of use', 'Copyright statement' or 'Legal terms'. Read this information carefully to find out if you can use an asset. Unless it says that reuse is allowed, you will need to ask permission or look for an alternative. Sometimes assets can be used as you find them, but you are not allowed to adapt them.

Professional multimedia authors and TV producers also have to ask (and pay) for the right to use assets such as music clips and photographs. If you need to ask permission to use something, politely explain how and why you wish to use the asset. Often you will be given permission to reuse the asset without any payment, especially if it is for educational purposes. However, this can be a lengthy process.

TALKING POINT 4.1

You need to find some images and adapt them for use in your products. Look at these notices from different websites. Which would allow you to do this?

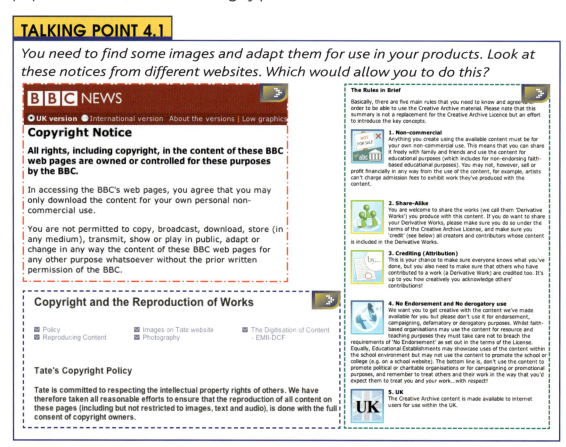

Acknowledgements

Whenever you use an asset from a secondary source, you should acknowledge the author or source of the material in your product. The same rules apply if you use an asset produced by one of your friends: you must still acknowledge the source.

Warning! **You must have permission from the author or owner of an asset. It is not acceptable to give the search engine you used to find it as the source.**

Keeping a record

Once you have a detailed design for a product, you will know exactly what assets you need. Your list of assets is likely to include:

► images
► animations
► video clips
► audio clips
► text.

But where will you get these from?

To save time, it makes sense to use assets from secondary sources and adapt them if necessary. Wherever it is appropriate, you should repurpose assets by using them in more than one product.

You must check that you have permission and acknowledge your sources correctly in your products. To do this properly, you need to keep a record of each asset as you gather it. This table shows what details you must include, but you may also want to include other information such as the type of multimedia.

Look at the range of different types of asset in this showcase.

Asset (file name and extension)	Type (primary or secondary)	Author (who produced it)	How much is used	What needs changing	Where it is used	Why it is used	Permission (is permission required and has it been obtained)
School.jpg	P	Myself	Whole image	–	'About our school' page	To show school as it is now	No permission needed
old lesson.mov	S	British Pathé	10 seconds	Compress	'History of school' page	To show a lesson from the fifties	Clip is licensed to be used in school

►► Activity 4.1

Create a file to store details of your assets for The Project. You could use this template or any other suitable method.

Gathering assets from secondary sources

If you know where to look, you can find a lot of high-quality material available that you don't have to pay for. Some websites offer free assets for students in schools and colleges.

There is now an international licensing scheme called Creative Commons, which encourages people who create their own digital assets to share them with others. On its website you will find links to many examples of high-quality still images, moving images and audio. The idea behind Creative Commons is that everyone can use – and in certain cases adapt – the original assets to create something new.

Finding images

Many people looking for an image start by using a search engine such as Google, which has an 'Image Search' facility.

However, there are drawbacks to this. Often search engines don't distinguish between copyright and non-copyright images. Most of the images you will find are likely to be protected by copyright. It is also likely that many of them are too small or of poor quality.

Creative Commons is one good source of images, but you can also find 'public domain' images. These are images that are not protected by copyright law. You can use any public domain image (or other type of asset that is in the public domain), although you still need to acknowledge where it came from. Many software packages include images that you can use provided that you own a licensed copy of the software.

Can I do this?

Using suitable ICT tools, make sure you can:

Download images from the internet

Use clipart and library images

▸▸ Activity 4.2

Look at your designs for THE PROJECT. Use secondary sources to look for images you need (legally!). What images could you repurpose? What images will you need to create yourself? Start to make entries in your assets file.

Finding videos and animations

There are a number of schemes in the UK that allow students to download and use moving images. These are often run by local education authorities, so ask if your school or college is part of one of these schemes.

The BBC has recently made a number of film clip resources available through the Creative Archive project.

The Creative Archive lets you preview stills from the video asset and also provides a full description

You may be able to access sources such as British Pathé News

Internationally, there are sites such as the Prelinger Archive which host thousands of film clips that you can use. It is likely that many similar sites will be set up in the future.

When you decide to download a moving image clip, check that the size (often given as pixels, for example 240 x 320) and format are suitable for your requirements.

Some sites, such as the Creative Archive, offer clips in several formats. You will need to find the one that will work best with your chosen multimedia authoring software.

Make sure you download in the most appropriate format

Can I do this?

Using suitable ICT tools, make sure you can:

Download video clips and animations from the internet

▶ Activity 4.3

Look at your designs for THE PROJECT. Use secondary sources to look for any video footage and animations you need. What could you repurpose? What will you need to create yourself? Remember to keep a record in your assets file.

Finding audio assets

Many excellent multimedia products produced by students unintentionally break copyright law. This is because they include music copied from their CD collections or downloaded from the internet.

However, as with the other media, there is a surprising amount of 'free' audio resources available. These include sound effects, speeches and performed music. The Creative Commons website is a good starting point. Other sites, such as Freeplay Music, offer clips of different lengths to download, which makes them ideal for use in your multimedia products. However, note that these clips are only for student, in classroom, use.

▶▶ Activity 4.4

Use secondary sources to look for audio assets you need for THE PROJECT. What could you repurpose? What will you need to create yourself? Keep a record!

Finding text assets

The same rules apply to using text from secondary sources. You cannot simply copy and paste someone else's text into your own products. You may be able to reword the text, but if not you must check whether you need to seek permission.

Some text will be in the form of images or animations – these can add interest to your products, but again you need to be sure you can use them. It may be simpler to create your own using suitable multimedia tools.

The Sky News website uses animated as well as standard texts.

▶▶ Activity 4.5

Use secondary sources to look for text assets for THE PROJECT. Can you use them? Do they need rewording or editing? What could you repurpose? With text, it is easy to forget to keep a record, but you must!

Using the right tools

For word processing, we have word processing software. Similarly, for presentations or databases there are specialist packages. But multimedia authoring uses a whole range of different software tools – word processing, web authoring, presentation, graphics, video editing and movie making, to name just a few. So when we talk about multimedia authoring software, what we really mean is a selection of any suitable software tools.

Images

Creating digital images is easy, but making sure they are fit for purpose takes a little longer! You can take photographs with a digital camera or use a scanner to capture pictures, artwork, maps and diagrams which you can then edit. You could even use a digital microscope or webcam.

When you capture your images, make sure that they are:

- the right size and resolution for the multimedia product you are creating
- saved in a format that will work with your web or multimedia authoring software – JPEG, GIF and PNG files are all suitable.

The kit

If you need to take photographs, you obviously need a camera, but don't worry if you don't have access to expensive equipment. You can get good enough images with a:

- mobile phone
- camcorder
- webcam
- digital camera
- scanner (to capture all types of existing images).

Resolution

Multimedia products are usually presented on some sort of screen. Most screens have a resolution of between 72 and 96 pixels per inch (ppi). Each pixel in an image equals one dot on the screen, so there will be 72 or sometimes 96 dots for every inch on the screen. There is no point in using images with a higher resolution than this. You will just end up with file sizes that are very large, which is a problem if users need to download them.

Taking digital photos

Always take more pictures than you think you need. It is better to do this than to have to go back and take more. Remember that digital pictures don't have developing costs, so you can afford to experiment.

TALKING POINT 4.2

Think about the photographs you need to take for THE PROJECT. Discuss why the following are important:

- going out on a bright sunny day with good light
- using a tripod
- taking more than one picture
- taking pictures from different viewpoints
- having enough memory in your camera
- reading the instruction booklet for your camera.

Make sure that your photos:

- ▶ are clear, with good colour or tone and contrast
- ▶ are well framed and composed
- ▶ contain images that make the point you want to make.

TALKING POINT 4.3

Look at these images. Which one do you prefer? What if the purpose is to illustrate an article about the tower in a local history book? What if it is for a book about the local area?

Look at the Kodak website for more tips.

Think carefully about the composition of your pictures – it will depend on the audience and purpose

Editing images

You will need to edit images from both primary and secondary sources. The file sizes need to be kept down so that download time is acceptable and your eportfolio conforms to the technical specification. You can do this by cropping an image to reduce its size (not by resizing it) or by reducing the resolution. When you optimise an image using either of these methods, you need to get the balance right between file size and quality.

Before editing …

… and after

Can I do this?

Using artwork and imaging software, make sure you can:

Use a digital camera   **Use a scanner**

Modify images   **Optimise images**

Group images   **Align and rotate images**

▶▶ Activity 4.6

Take some photos for THE PROJECT. Optimise each one to make it fit for its intended purpose. Save the original versions so that you can repurpose them.

This section has concentrated on photographs, but remember that there are many other types of image you can use – drawings, diagrams and logos to name just a few.

Video

You are not expected to produce full-length feature films for this unit! You can squeeze a surprising amount of information into a 30-second clip. Most TV adverts are about this length. They work because the individual shots they are made up of are very short, often lasting only a few seconds. If video shots are too long they will probably bore the audience.

TALKING POINT 4.4

Discuss your favourite TV adverts. What do you like about them? Is it the images, the music or the dialogue? How many shots has the director used in making each advert?

The kit

As with capturing images, you don't need the best digital video equipment for this course. Whatever you use, make sure you know how to set it up before you go out on a shoot.

For the camera, if the quality is good enough you can use a:

- camcorder
- mobile phone
- webcam.

You will also need a tripod and *ideally* an external microphone.

Look at the problems in this clip

Filming tips

Before setting out to film, don't forget to:

- check your equipment is in good working order
- take a tripod (essential for steady shots)
- take a microphone
- make sure batteries are charged and you have a spare.

If you take these simple precautions, you should avoid having to retake the footage.

Most of the rules that apply to creating still images also apply to video, but there are some extra things you need to remember:

- take a few seconds' extra footage at the beginning and end of a shot – this will make editing easier
- film in good light
- use a tripod to keep your camcorder steady
- don't film directly into the light – for example, avoid filming someone sitting in front of a window, unless they want to be anonymous
- don't zoom in and out – it makes the audience feel seasick!

Can I do this?

Using digital sound and video equipment, make sure you can:

Capture video

▶▶ Activity 4.7

Produce a video clip aimed at teenagers showing aspects of recycling in your school or college for use in THE PROJECT. The content can be anything for which video is appropriate. Concentrate on filming movement of people rather than static buildings. Try filming from different angles and positions. Use the built-in microphone. Import the footage onto your computer.

Sound

Most movies use sound of one sort or another. You can use voiceovers, special effects or music, or perhaps a mixture. Next time you watch a trailer, turn off the sound. Was the trailer effective without sound? What sound makes the trailer more effective?

Although many camcorders have built-in microphones, they often give poor results. For instance:

▶ in windy weather they pick up lots of hissing and rumbling
▶ when groups are speaking it can be difficult to pick out individual voices
▶ in quiet moments the camcorder motor can be heard.

You can avoid these problems by using an external microphone. You can also add sound at the editing stage.

This clip has lots of sound problems too!

Editing video

When you have finished filming you can use video editing software to create your movie sequence. Simple drag-and-drop techniques allow you to:

▶ arrange the shots on a timeline
▶ trim unwanted parts from the shots
▶ add transitions between some shots to change how they blend together
▶ add titles, subtitles and credits
▶ add sound and music.

Can I do this?

Using digital sound and video software, make sure you can:

Edit video　　　　　　　　　**Edit a video sound track**

Capture a video sound track　　**Remove a video sound track**

▶▶ Activity 4.8

Edit the video footage you captured in Activity 4.7. Edit the soundtrack and add titles that make the movie fit for audience and purpose.

Encoding

Digital video generates very large files. One minute of video can be up to 200MB. This would be far too large to use in your eportfolio.

Once you have finished editing you need to make the file size smaller and convert it so that it will play in your multimedia authoring software. This is called encoding. Encoding usually compresses the video to a smaller file size. Most digital video editing software has dialogue boxes and wizards to help you encode and convert your digital video file.

Encoding using two types of digital video editing software

Once you have encoded your video, the dimensions on screen will probably be smaller than the original and there will inevitably be some loss of quality. You have to make choices that balance quality, file size and video length.

Look at the movie at different resolutions

Can I do this?

Using digital sound and video software, make sure you can:

Encode a video clip

▶▶ Activity 4.9

Experiment with encoding to see if you can reduce the size of the video clip you edited in Activity 4.8 to less than 2.5MB.

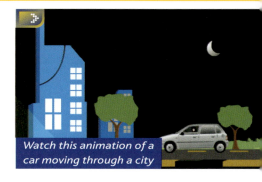

Watch this animation of a car moving through a city

Animations

Producing an effective animation can be very time-consuming. Allow plenty of time if you want to include this type of asset in your products.

There are two types of animation commonly used in multimedia: animated GIFs and vector animations.

Animated GIFs

GIF animations are generally made up of a set of images, called frames, which are placed on a timeline. These are displayed one after the other in a sequence to give the impression of movement. The images can be photographs, drawings or diagrams. You can set the time for which each frame displays and the number of times the whole animation should play. Animated GIFs are often used for pictures, buttons and banners.

Animated GIFs can be converted to movie and other file formats – this will depend on how you want to publish the animation. It might run on its own or be embedded in another product.

GIF animation made up of 44 frames

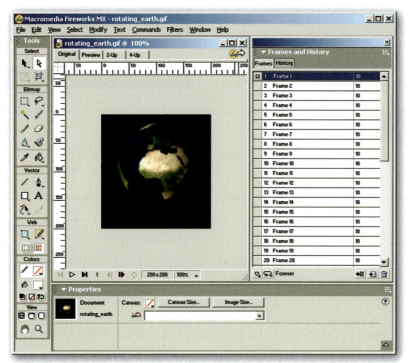

Most image editing software will allow you to create an animated GIF based on a timeline.

Vector animations

A vector graphic is created using software – it is not made of pixels. Like GIF animations, vector animations are created using timelines. The file sizes are very small and software can add movement and changes of shape and colour automatically. This has made the format very popular in multimedia and on websites.

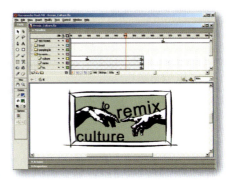

You can define the path that each object will follow across the screen and the time it will take. Vector animations have the ability to 'stream' so that a user can start viewing an animation while the rest of it is still downloading. Users need a browser plug-in to view them, but these are freely available.

> ## ▸▸ Activity 4.10
>
> **Carry out a web search for multimedia animation. Find some examples of GIF and vector animation. Compare and describe the differences between them.**

Can I do this?

Using artwork and imaging software, make sure you can:

Create animations   **Add user control**

Publish animations

> ## ▸▸ Activity 4.11
>
> **Experiment with the animation tools you have available. Produce any animations that you have included in your designs for THE PROJECT.**

Audio

An audio asset can be a voiceover, a narrative commentary, music or other sound effect. It can be a live recording or something you prepare at the computer, but in either case it is likely to need editing.

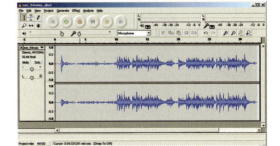

The kit

You will need to use:

► a headset or USB microphone
► a computer keyboard
► a music keyboard.

Recording audio

You can record audio by plugging a microphone into your computer, or you can use a portable device, such as a mini-disc recorder or an iPod with a microphone attachment.

Another option is to use software to record the sound from another source such as a CD or radio or by downloading from the internet.

Editing audio

If you include audio in multimedia products, you need to make sure the quality is as good as possible. Editing can vary from a simple task such as trimming audio clips to the right length to manipulating the sound or removing background noise. Sometimes you may need to combine two sources of audio and mix them together or add multiple tracks.

Can I do this?

Using digital sound software, make sure you can:

Capture a sound clip　　　　　**Edit a sound clip**

▶ Activity 4.12

Record some commentary and some music and add these to the short video clip you made in Activity 4.8. Try using different speakers' voices and different types of music. How does this change the look and feel of the video?

Text

Text can be imported from a secondary source or another file, or it can be typed in directly using the multimedia authoring tools you have chosen. Remind yourself of the audience and purpose so that your writing style is appropriate.

Arial
Verdana
Trebuchet
Tahoma

Suitable screen fonts

Remember that your multimedia products will be screen-based and so any font you choose must work well on screen. For accessibility it is important to ensure that your text is resizable on screen.

Although the spelling and grammar checkers in word processing software are valuable aids, they are no substitute for carefully proofreading your text. Make sure that there are no factual errors or omissions. Always ask someone whose judgment you trust to give you feedback on your text. If it contains technical or factual information, ask someone who knows about the subject to check it.

Can I do this?

Using multimedia authoring tools, make sure you can:

Enter and import text　　　　　**Format and edit text**
Make text resizable

▶ Activity 4.13

Here are some examples of text from different multimedia products.

These are just some of the wild adventures that you can do with me. Do you think that you can keep up with me and my friends?

Only in the eyes of New Yorkers is Chicago this country's Second City. For in the Windy City, visitors will find culture and chaos, sports and skyscrapers, dramatic architecture and a diverse population.

Enter this text in suitable multimedia authoring software. Experiment with different fonts and sizes. Preview the page and check that the text is resizable.

Repurposing your assets

Once you have created and collected a set of digital assets, it is a good idea to reuse them in different ways. For example, an image can be cropped, its colours and shape can be changed, and its size can be reduced or enlarged. If you have made a movie it can be a product on its own, but it can also be incorporated into a web page or presentation.

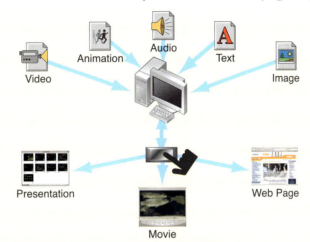

Once you have created a digital asset it is there for you to use as many times as you like. Sometimes you will need to adapt it

TALKING POINT 4.5

Look at these images of members of a cycling club. They are all produced from the same original photograph. What has been done to produce them? Can you think of suitable purposes for each?

▶▶ Activity 4.14

Select one of these images. Edit it so that you can use it in different ways. For example, crop it, change the colours, change its shape or use special effects. How could you make it suitable for use as a vertical panel on one side of a web page or as a background?

Tackling **THE PROJECT**

Preparing your assets

P

It's now time to prepare all the assets you need to build your products for **THE PROJECT**. First, you should go back and check your designs to make absolutely sure that you know what you need. Have you repurposed wherever you can to save time?

Don't forget that when you use a secondary source, you need to find out who the owner is and get permission if necessary.

Use the assets file you created earlier to keep a detailed record of the assets as you source them. Save the assets in the appropriate folders in your directory structure.

You could prepare all the assets of a particular type before moving on to the next type.

If you alter an asset in any way for use in a different product, remember to save it with a different file name so that you don't lose the original version. Use clear file names – for example, if you have a picture of a dustbin lorry called 'lorry.jpg' and you reduce the resolution for another product, you could add '_lowres' to the end of the file name and call it 'lorry_lowres.jpg'.

Have you got everything you need?

5 Building multimedia products

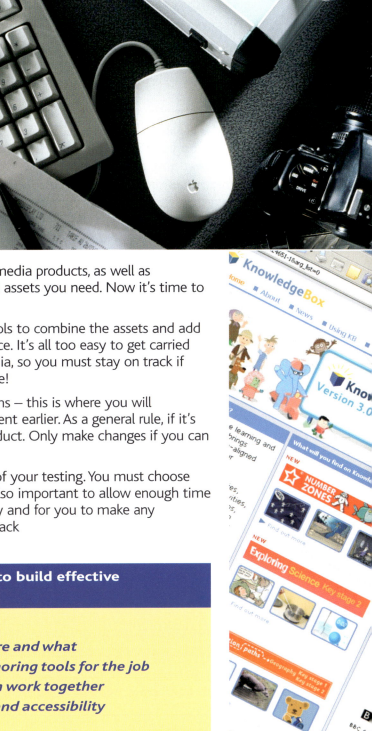

You have planned and designed your multimedia products, as well as gathering, creating and preparing the digital assets you need. Now it's time to build and test your products.

You'll need to use multimedia authoring tools to combine the assets and add interactivity to enhance the user's experience. It's all too easy to get carried away when you are working with multimedia, so you must stay on track if your products are going to be fit for purpose!

The trick is to make good use of your designs – this is where you will appreciate the value of all that time you spent earlier. As a general rule, if it's not in the design, it shouldn't be in the product. Only make changes if you can justify them.

The other key success factor is the quality of your testing. You must choose the right people to give you feedback. It's also important to allow enough time in your plan for them to do the job properly and for you to make any necessary changes as a result of their feedback

In this chapter you will learn how to build effective multimedia products by:

► *making use of your designs*
► *reminding yourself who, why, where and what*
► *selecting the best multimedia authoring tools for the job*
► *combining assets and making them work together*
► *addressing interactivity, usability and accessibility*
► *prototyping and testing*
► *making use of feedback*

5 Don't get carried away!

At last it's the moment you've been waiting for. It's time to start building your products! You have a set of assets for use in a product. Now you can combine them and make sure that they work together as they should. Don't lose sight of what the purpose is and keep asking yourself:

- ▶ Who is the product for?
- ▶ Why is it needed?
- ▶ Where will it be used?

WHY WHERE
WHO WHAT
HOW

If you have done a good job, your designs will tell you everything you need to know about the product, including what must go in it. You must follow your design carefully unless you find a good reason not to.

Sometimes you will have to sacrifice some of the work you have done already because you find that it is not suitable. However, you should never include something extra at this stage just because you like it or you have worked hard to produce it.

TALKING POINT 5.1

Why do you think a final product might not match its design? Is it worth spending all that time on design if you can change your mind at this stage? How would you record any changes you make to your designs?

Before you start, a word of caution. A DiDA student who spends all his spare time at the BMX club might be tempted to include images of bikes wherever he can in his eportfolio. Another might want to ignore the fact that a movie is far too long because she has spent the whole weekend producing it.

If bikes are not relevant, they shouldn't be there. If your design includes a 30-second movie clip, that's how long it must be in the product. Save the whole asset, as you never know when you might get a chance to repurpose it, but create an edited version to go in your product.

You must be firm with yourself – every single asset has to have a purpose and be fit for that purpose.

▶▶ Activity 5.1

Look at your design for the information point for THE PROJECT. Make sure that you have all the assets you need in the right folders and that they match your designs. Have you got any assets that you don't need?

Using multimedia authoring tools

In this chapter we will look at how you build products that combine multimedia assets with interactive components, such as buttons and hyperlinks. Although we will concentrate on three particular products, you can use the same techniques to build many others.

What tools can you choose from?

You can use different types of software to do the same job. For example, if you need to produce a scrolling presentation, you might think that the only option is to use presentation software. In fact, any software that allows you to combine assets on a timeline is worth considering.

You need to select tools that are suitable, but you must also think about which tools you have the skills to use. Don't try to learn how to use a package at the same time as working on a product – stick with what you know already!

However, you shouldn't simply choose the easiest option every time. Students are often tempted to use presentation software to build an information point because they think it is easy to use. In fact, there are far better tools for a fully interactive product like this.

TALKING POINT 5.2

What multimedia authoring tools are available in your centre? Which tools can you use confidently? Think of examples of products you could build with these tools.

▶▶ Activity 5.2

Working in groups, complete this table to show what software you have available in your centre. Decide which multimedia products each type of software could be used for.

Software name	Type of software	Which multimedia products could be built

5

Getting it right

Multimedia products can be entertaining, exciting, informative and much more besides, but they can also be a disaster if they don't work as they should! They are complex products so there are lots of things that can go wrong. The prototyping and testing process is always important, particularly when developing multimedia products.

Testing, testing!

Think about what you have done so far. You created some initial designs and asked for feedback. You developed a detailed design, checked it yourself and asked suitable people for comments to make sure that it was correct and complete. You have prepared a whole range of assets for your products and checked that they are what you need. All this is testing – making sure that you have done all you can at each stage.

So what's next? Nobody will want to use your product if it doesn't work properly. If you build a product, how will you know that it is fit for purpose?

Building a prototype

What are the chances of a multimedia product being right first time? In your project plans you should allow time for prototyping and testing. This involves producing working versions of your product at various stages during its development and testing them with users to make sure that they work. This gives you a chance not only to check that everything functions as it should, but also to find out whether your designs were right.

Always be critical of what you produce. You should go back and make improvements based on the feedback you receive. Don't worry if your final product doesn't match your design. What matters is that you keep a record of the feedback you receive and any changes you make as a result.

The production cycle

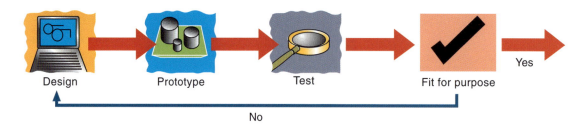

| Design | Prototype | Test | Fit for purpose | Yes |

No

This diagram says it all! Keep on getting feedback and making improvements until you are sure that the product is completely fit for purpose.

> ## ▸▸ Activity 5.3
>
> Look at this prototype of a virtual tour. It is aimed at tourists and its purpose is to encourage them to visit Hull. Is it fit for purpose? Can you spot anything obviously wrong with it? What feedback would you give?

Making products accessible and easy to use

Most multimedia products are designed to be used without help from those who produced them. There is no point in producing a product that some of your target audience will find difficult or impossible to use.

What are the needs of your target audience? Do you know? If you do, you can concentrate on their specific needs. If you don't, you should try to include as many features as you can to make the product accessible.

Maximise readability

► Make sure that links are easy to spot. Is it clear where they take the user? Text needs to be clear. 'More …' does not tell the user very much, does it?
► Don't only rely on colour.
► Make sure that fonts are resizable so that the user can increase or decrease the size themselves.
► Align content clearly. For example, if you have more than two lines of text, left align it, don't centre it.
► Use images, including symbols, to illustrate text.

Provide alternatives to visual content

► Provide alternative text for visual content, including images and symbols, animations and graphical buttons.
► If an image is a link, describe where the link goes rather than the image.
► Provide a description of video content.

Alternative text is used for images on this web page

Can I do this?

Using multimedia authoring software, make sure you can:

Add alternative text

▶▶ Activity 5.4

Explore the BBC website to find the features that are included for people who cannot see the screen clearly.

Provide alternatives to audio

If you include an audio file or a video clip which contains essential information for the user, you should also provide a transcript.

▶▶ Activity 5.5

Look at the prototype of the Hull virtual tour again. What features does it include to improve usability and accessibility? How could it be improved?

▶▶ Activity 5.6

Open this file and save its contents to a folder. Open the index.htm file using the tools you use for producing web pages. Add accessibility features to the page. Preview the page in your browser and ask others for comments.

Making products interactive

Different levels of interactivity

If you have designed a fully interactive product, such as an information point or virtual tour, the user will be able to move around it freely, visiting pages or screens in any order. The user is in complete control.

However, some products allow only limited interactivity. For example, in a quiz the route the user takes depends on the answers they give.

> **TALKING POINT 5.3**
>
> *Not all multimedia products are interactive. Think of some examples. Do you think that adding interactivity would enhance the user's experience? If so, how?*

Choosing the tools for interactivity

The level of interactivity required is an important factor in deciding which multimedia authoring tools to use. Presentation software is not the ideal package to produce fully interactive products. It would be better to use web authoring software.

However, presentation software is a good choice for products with limited interactivity, such as a quiz or interactive story. This type of software is designed for presentations, which are sequential products with links to visit related files on the way through.

▸▸ Activity 5.7

Look at the products in the Hull showcase. Evaluate the interactivity in each product. What about the interactivity of the showcase itself?

▸▸ Activity 5.8

Double check your structure chart and design notes for your information point. Make sure that you are happy with the interactivity offered to users.

Do the same for your quiz.

Using web authoring tools to build an information point

Web authoring tools lend themselves to producing products that have a high degree of interactivity. We are focusing on building an information point, but don't forget that the same tools can be used for many other products including virtual tours, websites, e-learning packages and, of course, eportfolios.

Organisation

Before you build a product using web authoring software, you must make sure that everything you want to include is stored inside the main folder for the product. This is very important when it comes to creating links, as you will know from your work in Unit 1.

> ## ▶▶ Activity 5.9
>
> **Check that you have a logical folder structure for your information point.**
> **Make sure all the assets you have prepared are stored in the correct folders.**

There are a number of ways you can build an information point. Here, we will begin by creating a page template and then use this to produce content pages. Once all the pages have been created, the page template will be updated by adding the correct links.

Page template

Using a template gives a product a consistent look and feel. You must ensure that a page template contains all the features that you want to appear on every screen — and nothing else.

TALKING POINT 5.4

Explore this virtual tour from the Hull showcase. Look at the screens. Are they consistent? What about navigational aids such as buttons? Are the same fonts and colours used throughout? If not, does it matter?

Can I do this?

Using multimedia authoring software, make sure you can:

Create a page template	**Format and edit text**
Use a table for page layout	**Include multimedia assets**
Build a navigation bar	**Create interactive buttons**

> ## ▶▶ Activity 5.10
>
> **Using suitable web authoring tools, create a site for your information point. Create your page template, including the navigation bar and interactive buttons. Use your storyboard to guide you. You will not be able to add the links to your navigation bar just yet.**

Content pages

Once you have a template, you can build the other pages in your product. Each page will consist of a combination of assets that you have already prepared. Follow your storyboard and base each page on the template. If you change the template, the software will update all the other pages.

Can I do this?

Using web authoring tools, make sure you can:

Add an image to a web page   **Crop and resize images**

Align images   **Add lines and shapes**

Colour images   **Use colours**

▸▸ Activity 5.11

Using suitable web authoring tools, create each of the content pages for your information point. Use your storyboard to help you and make sure that each page is based on the page template.

Making the connections

The next stage is to create all the links in a product. Links enable users to move around the product. You don't want users to find themselves stuck on a page unable to move on.

Explore the different types of link used on this website

Can I do this?

Using web authoring tools, make sure you can:

Use hyperlinks to link pages   **Create interactive rollovers**

Create interactive text links   **Create interactive hotspots**

▸▸ Activity 5.12

Continue working on your information point using your storyboard and structure chart to guide you. Create the links in your page template and update all the content pages. Add the links, hotspots and buttons to the contents pages. Check that all the links go where they should.

How have you indicated that there is a link on a page? If you have used buttons or images, remember to include alternative text as well. Make sure that it is quite clear what each link is for and where it will take the user.

Testing it yourself

Does it work?

The next stage involves looking at the product as a whole. You must make sure that it works as intended. Before you start, you should look back at the original requirements and remind yourself of the who, why, where, what and how for the product.

You need to make sure that the product meets the needs of the audience and purpose by checking:

- ► Is the content correct?
  - ▷ Is it accurate?
  - ▷ Does it convey the right messages?

- ► Do all the links and hyperlinks work as intended?
  - ▷ Do they go where they should?
  - ▷ Are they all working?

- ► Are all the interactive features working?
  - ▷ Hotspots?
  - ▷ Rollovers?
  - ▷ Buttons?

- ► Does the product work in a range of different browsers?

Is it user-friendly?

You will help your users if your navigation is clear and consistent.

- ► Are links and buttons obvious to the user? Is it clear where the links go?
- ► Is the navigation bar in the same place on every page? If not, you haven't used your template properly!
- ► If you have included a map like this one, are the hotspots in sensible areas, do they work and do they enhance the user experience by providing further information?
- ► If you have included video or audio files, can the user control their use as intended, for example starting and stopping when they like?

How user-friendly is the navigation on this virtual tour?

Look at each check in the table and discuss what you need to do to test this properly. Complete the table so that you can use it to help you test your information point.

Checks	Activities
Is the content correct?	
Do all the links work and go where they should?	
Does the interactivity work properly?	
Does it work in different browsers?	

Using a log to track changes

It is a good idea to keep a record of the changes you make as a result of testing. Here is a sample log sheet you might like to use for your alpha test.

Issue	Problem	Action taken/recommended
Navigation	After leaving the home page had to use browser back button to get back to the home page.	Insert buttons to return to the home page on each subsequent page.
Functionality	Link to video not working.	Correct the link.
Language	Difficult terms (jargon) are not explained in the text.	Create hyperlinks to a glossary for difficult terms or jargon.
Feedback	When users complete one of the interactive elements they get no feedback.	Build in feedback loop.
Consistency	Different fonts and different font sizes are used throughout the site.	Standardise fonts throughout.

A sample log for alpha testing

▸▸ Activity 5.13

Test your information point using the activities you discussed in Talking Point 5.5. Keep a log of the problems you find. You could use a table like the one above.

Once you are happy with your product, is that it? Of course not! You will not be the one using it. There will be more on this later.

You haven't finished your information point yet, but you have got a first prototype. As a class, look at each prototype in turn. Discuss how it looks and feels to the user. What needs to be done to improve it?

Using presentation tools to create a quiz

Presentation software can be used for far more than standard presentations. Here we will use it to produce a multimedia quiz with limited interactivity. The way in which users can move around will depend on the answers they give. Users cannot go wherever they like as they can in an information point.

In Chapter 3 you looked at flowcharts for quiz design and you produced one for THE PROJECT. This shows the different paths a user can take through the quiz. If the quiz is to work, navigation aids must be clear, pages must be linked together and it should always be possible to get back to the start.

TALKING POINT 5.7

What are the limitations of using presentation software to produce a quiz? Can you keep a score? Can you allow users to watch a video clip more than once or to pause an audio clip? What other multimedia features might you want to build into a quiz?

Organisation

Before you build a quiz, you must make sure that all the assets are stored in the correct folder.

▶ Activity 5.14

Check that you have a logical folder structure for your quiz. Make sure all the assets you have prepared are stored in the correct folders.

Creating the slides

You should use a master slide to control the look of your slides. The master slide is a template that contains all the features used on every slide, including:

► font styles
► placeholders (boxes to hold a title, text, charts, tables or pictures)
► colour schemes
► background designs.

Can I do this?

Using presentation tools, make sure you can:

Create a master slide	**Format text**
Create and use colour schemes	**Include multimedia assets**
Use frames	**Align images**
Create interactive rollovers	**Create interactive buttons, text links and hotspots**
Add lines and shapes	**Colour images**
Crop and resize images	

▶▶ Activity 5.15

Using presentation tools, create your master slide and content slides. Use your storyboard to guide you.

Custom animation

Your designs will have included some animated objects. For each one, you will need to set the start and finish points, the type of animation and timings.

Making the connections

The next stage is to create all the links. In a quiz, this is quite complex because each question has more than one possible response and each answer must take the user to the appropriate slide. Using your flowchart will you help to get this right.

Transitions

Transitions control how one slide changes to the next. You will need to set the type of transition, the timing and how it is triggered. This can happen automatically after a set time or on an instruction, such as a mouse click.

Can I do this?

Using presentation tools, make sure you can:

Create links

Create custom animations

Create slide transitions

▶▶ Activity 5.16

Using your designs, add all the links, animations and transitions to your quiz.

Testing, testing!

Testing a quiz is not as simple as it might seem. You must check every possible path that a user could take. This is where a flowchart comes in handy!

TALKING POINT 5.8

When you test a quiz, you must check that:
- ▶ *the animations work correctly*
- ▶ *the timings are right*
- ▶ *the transitions take the user from one slide to the next smoothly.*
What else do you need to check?

▶▶ Activity 5.17

Use your flowchart to check that your quiz works as you intended. Check that the user can move on only by clicking on a link and not just anywhere on the screen.

What do other people think?

You must try out your products on users who are representative of the target audience. This stage is crucial and means that you will gather constructive feedback. It can highlight shortcomings in a product that you failed to spot. This is often because you are too familiar with it.

The main things you need to find out are:

▶ Can other people use the product without help?
▶ Do other people understand how the product works?
  ▷ Is it clear how to navigate through the product?
  ▷ Are the interactive elements clear?
  ▷ Do they know what they are trying to achieve?
▶ What do other people like about the product?
▶ What do other people dislike about the product and why?
▶ Are there any changes users would like to see in addition to those you have already made?

TALKING POINT 5.9

Who should you ask to test your product? You don't want someone who will just be nice about it. You need people who will try to break it! What information does a test user need to have to do the job properly?

Usability tests

A usability test involves giving test users a set of instructions and watching how they carry them out using your product. They should be invited to comment as they go along.

You need to:

▶ Identify a task you want your test user to undertake, e.g. to find their way around the information point in a particular order.
▶ Make sure they are clear about what you are asking them to do.
▶ Record their actions, concerns or comments (see below).
▶ Observe what test users do as they work through your product. Record any comments or problems on the logging sheet as they arise.
▶ Try not to prompt your users or help them too much. If they cannot find their way around your product you need to know this, rather than intervening to show them where to go.

▶▶ Activity 5.18

Ask someone to use your quiz so that you can conduct a usability test. Make changes where necessary and then ask the same person to test the product again.

TALKING POINT 5.10

In what other ways could you test for usability?

How many people do you need to conduct a test?

You may be used to asking just one of your peers, or perhaps your teacher, to test your products. This really isn't enough for a multimedia product. There are so many things that could go wrong and one person is unlikely to find them all.

However, it is very important to use the same people throughout. If you get feedback from someone and make changes based on their comments, it makes sense to ask them what they think of the improved version. If you ask someone else, they will probably focus on completely different issues.

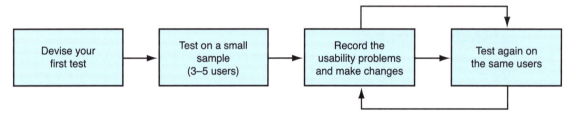

| Devise your first test | → | Test on a small sample (3–5 users) | → | Record the usability problems and make changes | → | Test again on the same users |

▸▸ Activity 5.19

Carry out a usability test on your information point. Select suitable people to test the product and record their comments. Make changes where necessary and then ask the same people to test the product again.

Proof of testing

The quality of a final product tells you how effective the testing has been. When it comes to the SPB, the moderator does not need to see every mistake you made and what you did to correct it. Students often spend far too long producing this type of evidence and then don't have time to make sure that the product actually works.

This does not mean that you can skimp on testing – if you do, the moderator will find out! However, you should keep a note of feedback you receive and improvements you make so that you can write a really good commentary for each product and talk about your experiences in your review.

Don't forget that your eportfolio is a multimedia product too and needs to be just as carefully tested if you want to keep the moderator happy!

Sit back and view!

Some multimedia products are not interactive. Apart from starting, stopping and pausing them, users just sit back and view the action.

For a non-interactive product to be successful, it must grab the user's attention and keep it. You must think carefully about how long it should be. If it is too long, people will not watch it to the end. If there is not enough to keep their attention, they may get bored.

TALKING POINT 5.11

When you carry out a usability test on a non-interactive product such as a movie or scrolling presentation, what will you be looking for?

Which tools should you use?

There is a lot of software that can be used to create non-interactive products, such as movies. This ranges from utilities included with your computer operating system to sophisticated commercial packages.

Any software that allows you to place assets on separate layers and make them start and stop independently of one another is suitable.

TALKING POINT 5.12

What software is available to you for creating and editing movies? What are the pros and cons of each package?

Get organised!

You must make sure that everything you want to include is stored inside the main folder for the product.

▶▶ Activity 5.20

Check that you have a logical folder structure for your movie for THE PROJECT. Make sure all the assets you have prepared are stored in the correct folders.

Timeline and layers

Your storyboard will include a number of layers on a timeline. You need to use your storyboard to help you create the right layers for the product. Remember to use sensible names for the layers.

Frames

You will need to check your design to see how many frames you need so that you create exactly the right number for your product.

HULL MOVIE

| 2 Sec | 4 Sec | 6 Sec | 8 Sec | 10 Sec | 12 Sec | 14 Sec | 16 Sec | 18 Sec |

Frames or scenes of the movie	Title	Scene 1	Scene 2	Scene 3	Title	Scene 4	Scene 5	Title
	Halt at Hull	Flags.jpg	Anchor.jpg	Sign.jpg	Relax in Trinity Square	Trinity_1.jpg	Trinity_2.jpg	The Deep
Transitions								
Audio	Audio track will be a voiceover*							
Music Track	Music track will be guitar music with a strong beat							
Overlay Track		Welcome to Hull						

* See separate document for script of voiceover.

All transitions are a slow fade.

Can I do this?

Using multimedia authoring tools, make sure you can:

Add layers to a timeline   **Add transitions**

Use frames   **Add titles and overlays**

Add assets to a timeline   **Publish a movie**

▶▶Activity 5.21

Using your storyboard to guide you, create a timeline for your movie for THE PROJECT. Create the layers and set the number of frames you need.

Putting the assets on the timeline

The next stage is to add each asset to the correct layer and make sure that it starts and stops in the right place. Add in the actions and transitions you planned.

▶▶Activity 5.22

Build your movie by placing the assets on the timeline and then adding actions and transitions.

Use the preview features in your software to make sure that everything works and fits together as you planned. As you work, remember to keep checking that the movie matches the design and that the timings work.

Does it work?

Remember how important it was to prototype and test an interactive multimedia product. It's no less important for a non-interactive product, such as a movie, but it is a very different process. You need to test it in a similar environment to its proposed location. If your product will be viewed in a busy public place, will your audience be able to hear the sound?

Ask a test user to view the product without any introduction from you. Then discuss and make notes about their experience.

What did they see?

Does their description match what you intended them to see? Was there enough time to take it all in? Did the user overlook anything important in the content?

What did they hear?

Was the soundtrack clear? Did they understand the commentary? Did they like the music and any other sound effects?

How did it make them feel?

Did your user's experience match your expectations? If not, was this because there is something wrong with your design or did you pick an inappropriate test user?

What did they learn?

What information did you hope to convey? Were you successful? Were some messages more effective than others?

What do they think the movie is for?

If your intention was to make people aware of the need to save water but the user thinks it is about bathroom fittings, then there is something wrong!

This feedback will test your product from the audience's point of view.

The production process is a cycle: you create, test and refine until the publication is fit for audience and purpose.

Getting help

There is no doubt that building multimedia products is a tricky business. Where can you turn for help when you get stuck?

Who do you know? Is there someone in your group or centre who knows what they are doing? Have they solved a similar problem? Even if there is no one around who has had a similar problem, the chances are that someone has the answer.

You can also look on the internet for online tutorials, specialist forums and other sources of help.

▸▸ Activity 5.23

Search the internet for advice on creating multimedia products using the tools you have available. Try the manufacturers of the software first.

This website is another good source of software tutorials.

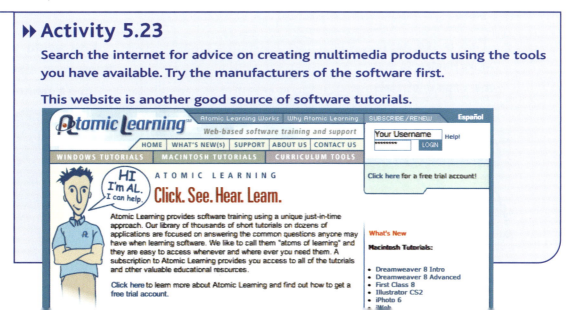

Tackling THE PROJECT

Now it's time to finish building each of your products. Review your work on the information point, quiz and movie. Have you fully tested each one? Would you be happy to publish them? If not, what else needs to be done?

Before you go any further, stop for a moment and remind yourself of a few important points that will help you to achieve your goal:

- remind yourself of the audience and purpose of each product
- keep referring to your designs as you go along
- produce prototypes
- check them for
  - accuracy
  - readability
  - consistency
  - usability
  - accessibility
  - interactivity
  - user experience
- use the production cycle and check fitness for purpose.

Remember that your aim is to create a multimedia experience for the users of your products.

Digital story

This is an interesting product. What tools will you use to produce it? Look at your designs and the assets you intend to include. What type of software will do the job? If you have designed a fully interactive product, web authoring software or something similar may be the right choice. If the product is more sequential with little or no interactivity, the choice is wider. It's up to you!

When it comes to testing, make sure that you involve test users who can represent the target audience.

Scrolling presentation

Don't be fooled into thinking that this is an easy product or that you must use presentation software. This unit is about using multimedia to enhance the user experience and your presentation must do just that. Looking back at your designs, you may decide that presentation software has all the tools you need to build the product, but you should also consider other options that will allow you to use a timeline.

6 Producing an eportfolio and reviewing your work

Now you've made it this far, it's time to build your eportfolio.

Remind yourself who it is for and why it is needed. You need to design it with the audience and purpose in mind.

You should see this as a chance to show off your ability to use multimedia. You can get your message across by producing an interactive showcase for your achievements.

If you have worked your way through this book, you will have all the skills you need to make a fantastic job of your eportfolio so that it really shows what you are capable of.

A word of advice before you start: allow plenty of time for prototyping and testing and don't be tempted to skip the design stage in favour of playing with the multimedia tools.

In this chapter you will learn how to build an interactive multimedia eportfolio by:

► *organising the content*
► *designing an appropriate structure*
► *using a template to ensure consistency*
► *including multimedia to enhance the user experience*
► *prototyping and testing to ensure fitness for purpose*

Haven't you done all this before?

Most of this chapter is about creating an eportfolio. You've already done Unit 1 and know how to build one, so why all the fuss? This time, you should think of the eportfolio as the ultimate multimedia product. More of this shortly, but first you need to get organised.

Getting organised

Before you start, have you got everything you need? Make sure that you have stored each item of evidence in the correct folder within a main folder for the eportfolio. You must be able to find things easily when you come to create the links.

Don't forget that you can include only file formats listed in the SPB. Now is the time to check and convert files if necessary. At the same time, check that you have compressed files where necessary so that your eportfolio stays within the maximum size limit. When you do the real SPB, check the list of file formats and the maximum size for the eportfolio as these may change from year to year.

Planning your eportfolio structure

As you know, there are many different possible structures for an eportfolio and you are free to come up with your own. What matters is that your structure is logical and that the user can find their way around it easily.

In this example, the evidence is divided into four main sections. Each of these sections will contain a number of content pages with commentaries and links to evidence.

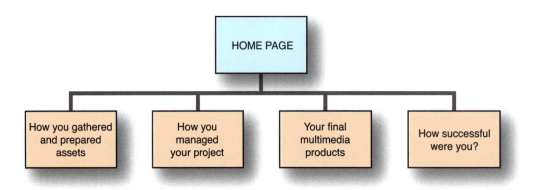

TALKING POINT 6.1

What do you think of the structure shown above? Does the software you are using for your eportfolio affect your choice of structure?

Whatever structure you decide on, bear in mind that users do not want to spend a long time trying to work out how to access any individual piece of evidence. The structure needs to be simple and consistent.

►► Activity 6.1

Produce a structure chart for your eportfolio showing how the pages will link together.

Making navigation clear

Visual links

Thumbnail images

On every page of your eportfolio you will need to include links to products and supporting information. Text links are one option, but you could also use images to provide a visual link to each item. For example, you could use a thumbnail image of the opening screen for each product.

Site map

Another idea is to produce a site map or similar diagram of your eportfolio with each item linking to the evidence.

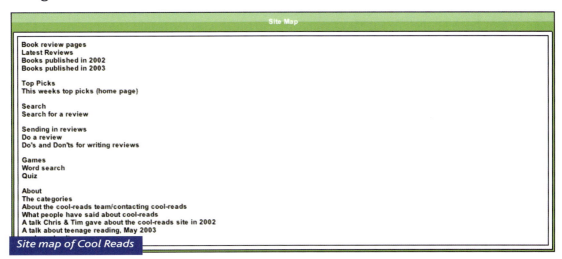

Site map of Cool Reads

Using a template

You have seen how useful templates are for consistency and you should use one for your eportfolio. Your template can include multimedia assets, such as an animated logo or image, if you want them to appear on every page.

A template is also a good way to ensure that your navigation bar remains consistent on all pages. Of course, another advantage of using a template is that if you decide to make any changes to the common areas, you only need to change the template. Any page that is based on that template will then be updated automatically.

Example of a template page for an eportfolio

▶▶ Activity 6.2

Design a page template for your eportfolio using a storyboard.

Enhancing the user experience

How can you put everything you have learned into practice and make best use of your multimedia skills? We will look at some ideas here, but always remember that you should not do things just for the sake of it – this usually puts the user off. If there is more than one multimedia component on a page, make sure only one thing happens at a time. A user cannot view or listen to more than one feature at once.

TALKING POINT 6.2

It is said that a user makes a decision about the quality of a website in the first ten seconds, which means just by looking at the first page. If this is true, it also applies to your eportfolio. Do you agree? Does your home page really matter that much?

Your home page

Your home page is your 'shop window'. How can you persuade the moderator that it is going to be a good experience to go inside and look around? Of course, you must include specified details, including your name, candidate number, centre name and number, but that's not very exciting, is it?

TALKING POINT 6.3

How can multimedia be used on the home page to enhance the moderator's experience? What might annoy or distract them?

Summary of contents

Your home page needs some sort of introduction to the eportfolio, what it's about and what is in it. A simple textual introduction is acceptable, but how else could you do it?

You could use images to illustrate the text. For example, your eportfolio for **THE PROJECT** might include a photograph of a landfill site or a still from your movie or information point.

If you really want to go to town you could include a movie trailer. This could take the user through the key areas of your eportfolio and persuade them to explore it further.

This student included a movie trailer on his homepage

Links

Assuming you have persuaded the user to look inside, how will they get to the evidence?

You may decide to include a navigation bar on every page, including the home page, or you may prefer to move to a contents page first. Either way, any links on the home page need to be clear and self-explanatory. Well-designed buttons or images will have a much better impact than plain text.

▶▶ Activity 6.3

Design the home page for your eportfolio, using a storyboard.

Commentaries

Each piece of evidence needs to be put into context. It's rather like the wrapping on an Easter egg – the packaging makes all the difference. Use your context pages to set the scene so that the moderator gets a really good idea of what you are presenting and how you achieved it. Keep your commentaries concise and to the point as the moderator will have to read them on screen. Don't forget to check that they are error-free. Think about how you can use multimedia assets to illustrate your comments.

It's a good idea to make notes as you work through a project so that you can include them in your commentaries.

TALKING POINT 6.4

These three context pages are intended to introduce a product in an eportfolio. What do you like and dislike about each one? How could they be improved? What would a moderator make of them?

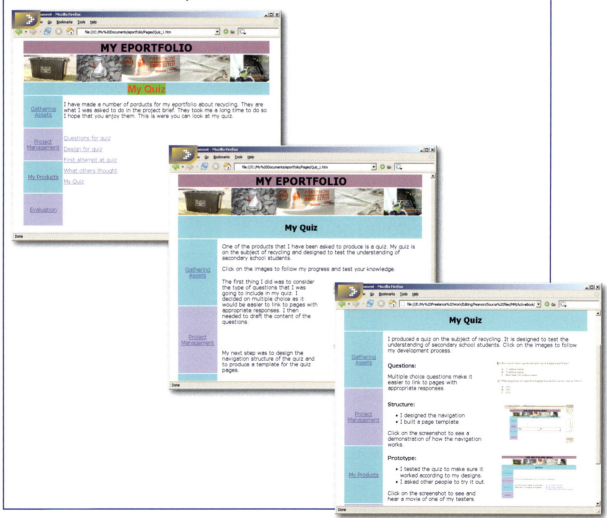

▶▶ Activity 6.4

Produce a storyboard for the context pages of your eportfolio. These should be based on your page template.

Making sure that links work

Don't be one of those students who uses the wrong types of links! Remind yourself of the difference between relative and absolute links. The rules are quite simple:

Relative links are used to link to other files within your eportfolio.
Absolute links are *only* used when you want to link to something outside the eportfolio, such as a website.

▸▸ Activity 6.5

Build your eportfolio using your structure chart and storyboard to help you. Make sure that all links to files within the eportfolio are relative, not absolute. If you can, check it on a stand-alone machine to make sure that all the links work.

Accessibility

You might know quite a lot about your assessor but you have no idea who the moderator is. You should include accessibility features in your eportfolio to make sure that the moderator has no trouble finding and viewing all the content. Revisit the information in Chapter 5 if you need to and make sure that your eportfolio is accessible.

▸▸ Activity 6.6

Add accessibility features such as alt-text if you haven't done so already. Check that fonts are resizable. Ask others to comment on the accessibility of your eportfolio.

Acknowledging sources

Make sure you have information about each of the assets used in your project. You should have collected this as you went along. Make sure you have a record of each asset, including:

- ▸ file name (including extension, for example cyclist.jpg)
- ▸ whether it came from a primary or secondary source
- ▸ description of the asset
- ▸ where you got it from
- ▸ who created the asset
- ▸ how you have adapted it
- ▸ where it was used
- ▸ copyright information.

Don't forget to include details of all the assets from both primary and secondary sources. You can only gain credit for the assets you have created yourself if you make clear what they are and where to find them.

▸▸ Activity 6.7

Make sure that you have fully acknowledged all the sources in your eportfolio for THE PROJECT, both primary and secondary. Check that you have not used other people's work without permission.

Project review

You must include a comprehensive project review in your eportfolio.

What should this include?

Your review should include feedback from others and cover all aspects of the project including:

- your multimedia products
- the project as a whole
- your own performance
- suggestions for improvement.

Don't just give a step by step description of everything you did. Try to pick out key points to comment on.

While you were designing and creating your assets and multimedia products you were collecting feedback from others. Now you need to get feedback on how you have performed in the project as a whole.

TALKING POINT 6.5

Listen to these audio clips. Two reviewers are giving feedback on a student's performance. Which one is most useful? Do you think the reviewers understood what they were being asked to do?

Reviewing your own performance

Reviewing your own performance is probably the hardest part of the review process, but it is something you will get better at with practice. You need to be really honest with yourself. The idea is to learn from your experiences.

▶▶ Activity 6.8

Listen to the two recordings of students who have just completed a multimedia project. They are talking about what they think they have learned from doing the project and what they might do differently next time. Compare the two accounts. Which one is more informative?

▶▶ Activity 6.9

Review your work on THE PROJECT, considering all the aspects listed above. Use multimedia tools where you can to present your review in a creative way. Add your review to your eportfolio and make sure that the links work.

Getting the size right

If you submit an eportfolio that is bigger than the maximum file size then it may not be accepted and all your work will be wasted. You must check the maximum allowed for the SPB you are working on. If you find yourself in trouble at this late stage, you MUST do something about it.

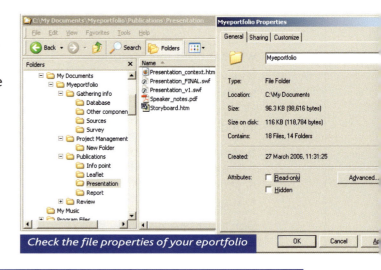

Check the file properties of your eportfolio

▶▶ **Activity 6.10**

Check the size of your eportfolio.

Prototyping and testing

This is one of the most important stages in the whole process. There is no point in spending hours on all those exciting multimedia products if the assessor and moderator can't get to them or if they don't work properly. Not only that, you need to make sure that your eportfolio has that 'feel good factor'.

Does it work properly?

You need to check that:

You don't want the moderator to see an error message like this!

- ► the content is correct, with
  - ▷ all the evidence and nothing unnecessary
  - ▷ the final version in each case, not an earlier one by mistake.
- ► the content works as intended
  - ▷ all products and supporting evidence display clearly on screen
  - ▷ each product works as intended when run from within the eportfolio
- ► the links and hyperlinks work as intended
  - ▷ all links go where they should
  - ▷ every item of content has a link to it
- ► all the interactive features work
  - ▷ hotspots
  - ▷ rollovers
  - ▷ buttons
- ► accessibility features work
  - ▷ alternative text
  - ▷ resizable fonts
- ► the product works in a range of different browsers.

Does it have the 'feel good factor'?

Have you made effective use of multimedia tools to showcase your achievements and enhance the user experience? You should check that:

- ▶ navigation is clear and consistent
  - ▷ links and buttons are easy to spot
  - ▷ it is clear where the links go
- ▶ the layout is clear and consistent
  - ▷ the navigation bar and other common features are in the same place on every page
  - ▷ pages are well laid out and not cluttered
- ▶ the eportfolio is fully interactive
  - ▷ users can control what they do next
  - ▷ users can control the use of video and audio assets as intended
  - ▷ multimedia assets encourage interactivity rather than distract the user
- ▶ the eportfolio is as accessible as possible
  - ▷ accessibility features are clear to the user.

TALKING POINT 6.6

Take each of these checks in turn and discuss what you need to do to test your eportfolio properly.

Who else should test your eportfolio?

You should know by now that it is not enough to test a product yourself. You can collect feedback from a wide range of different people including your peers, teachers and other adults. Remember that the audience for this particular product is the assessor and the moderator, so choose your test users carefully.

Use the checklists above to make sure that you get feedback on all the important issues.

Usability tests

It is certainly worth conducting a usability test so that you can get an idea of the experience the moderator will encounter.

Proof of testing

The quality of your eportfolio will tell the moderator and assessor everything they need to know about the effectiveness of your testing. You do not need to include evidence of corrections or improvements you make. However, you will need to talk about your experience of producing the eportfolio in your review, so it is worth keeping notes on problems you encountered and feedback you received.

As with other products, this does not mean that you can afford to spend less time on testing if you want to keep that moderator smiling!

6 Tackling **THE PROJECT**

Are you sure that your eportfolio for **THE PROJECT** is as good as it can be? Use this list to make sure that you've checked everything. Open the file and add more things that you should check. Compare your results with others in your group.

Checklist	Complete
Have you moved all your assets, products and other files into folders that are within the eportfolio structure?	☐
Have you tested all the links to make sure the navigation works as planned?	☐
Has someone else tested it for you? It would be a good idea to do this on another computer to make sure that you are not linking to evidence that falls outside the folder structure.	☐
Are all the file types acceptable?	☐
Have you checked that the total file size does not exceed the size permitted by the SPB? Where necessary, consider how to reduce file sizes.	☐
Is the eportfolio suitable for the target audience? Remember this is the assessor and the moderator.	☐
Are your pages attractive and consistent? Do they look as though they all belong to the same site?	☐
Is the text readable? Are the font size and style, the colour of text and the background suitable?	☐
Have you correctly acknowledged all sources?	☐
Have you carried out a review of the project and made this available within the eportfolio? Remember, the project should be reviewed by others and yourself.	☐
Can the assessor and the moderator navigate easily when looking for specific pieces of evidence? Make it easy for them to give you the marks.	☐

Test your eportfolio to make sure that it works both on your computer and on a standalone machine. Work in groups and test the final eportfolios for each other.

Skills list

Artwork and imaging software

Digital sound and video

Internet and intranets

Multimedia authoring software

Presentation software

Index